Hume on God

Continuum Studies in British Philosophy
Series Editor: James Fieser, University of Tennessee at Martin, USA

Continuum Studies in Continental Philosophy is a major monograph series from Continuum. The series features first-class scholarly research monographs across the field of British philosophy. Each work makes a major contribution to the field of philosophical research.

Hume on God
Irony, Deism and Genuine Theism

Timothy S. Yoder

continuum

Continuum International Publishing Group

The Tower Building
11 York Road
London SE1 7NX

80 Maiden Lane,
Suite 704
New York, NY 10038

www.continuumbooks.com

British Library Cataloguing-in-Publication Data

A catalogue record for this book is available from the British Library.

ISBN-10: HB: 1-8470-6146-X
ISBN-13: HB: 978-1-8470-6146-1

Library of Congress Cataloging-in-Publication Data

A catalog record for this book is available from the Library of Congress.

Typeset by Newgen Imaging Systems Pvt Ltd, Chennai, India
Printed and bound in Great Britain by MPG Biddles Ltd, King's Lynn, Norfolk

I dedicate this book, with love
and thanks, to my parents, Barry and Ruth Yoder.

Contents

Acknowledgments

This book has been a part of my life for nearly a dozen years now. Its humble beginnings were as the first research paper I wrote in my Philosophy graduate studies at Marquette University in Fall, 1997. Later, I had opportunity to present my findings at two conferences – for the Evangelical Philosophical Society in Orlando in 1998 and then at a meeting of the Society of Christian Philosophers in St. Paul in 2002. Eventually, it became my dissertation, which I defended in May, 2005. And now, thanks to the kind invitation of Jim Fieser, it finds new life as a book. It is a privilege to write about a great philosopher on the greatest of all possible topics – even if I do not agree with his conclusions!

It is a pleasant duty to acknowledge those individuals who have graciously provided me with the necessary assistance for this endeavor. The Philosophy faculty at Marquette has educated and shaped me, for which I am very thankful. I especially want to recognize William Starr, James South, Claudia Schmidt, Thomas Prendergast and Walter Stohrer, S.J. My fellow graduate students at Marquette have been just as influential on my development as a philosopher. Grateful thanks are given for hours of conversation and debate, and for continued friendship to Andrew Gustafson, Dan Kern, Jeff Goins, Michael Dougherty and Larry Masek.

I also want to express my gratitude to my faculty colleagues, my students and the administration at Philadelphia Biblical University, especially to the members of the School of Arts and Sciences for collegiality and to President Todd Williams for vision and leadership. I am also grateful to Nancy Painter for many tasks done graciously and efficiently. I have benefited from the editorial assistance provided by my father, Barry Yoder, my wife, Lisa and my colleague, Roselee Bancroft, as they read various chapters and made invaluable suggestions. I thank Tim Eimer for years of friendship, collaboration and insipiration. I have also benefited from the courteous and professional assistance of Sarah Campbell and Tom Crick at Continuum, for which I am very appreciative.

I am blessed with a wonderful family. My wife, Lisa, saw the completion of the long journey of this book, and did so with grace, love and a smile on her face. My parents have never stopped encouraging me through many long years of school. It was a thrill to be able to return home and to be a colleague with my father on the faculty of PBU for the last 5 years. My thanks are to God for truth, the universe and a mind to contemplate them both.

Abbreviations

I will cite passages from Hume's corpus in the text according to the following legend. The abbreviations for the Essays are those used by Claudia Schmidt in *David Hume: Reason in History*.

DNR (part. paragraph) *Dialogues concerning Natural Religion*, edited by Norman Kemp Smith (Indianapolis: Bobbs-Merrill, 1947).

E (essay title abbreviation, page) *Essays: Moral, Political, and Literary*, edited by Eugene F. Miller (2nd edition, Indianapolis: Liberty Fund, 1985).

EHU (section. part. paragraph) *An Enquiry concerning Human Understanding*, edited by Tom L. Beauchamp (Oxford: Oxford University Press, 2000).

EPM (section. part. paragraph) *An Enquiry concerning the Principles of Morals*, edited by Tom L. Beauchamp (Oxford: Oxford University Press, 1998).

H (volume. chapter. page) *The History of England*, edited by William B. Todd (Indianapolis: Liberty Fund, 1983).

L (letter number; volume number. page) *The Letters of David Hume*, edited by J. Y. T. Greig (Oxford: Clarendon Press, 1932).

LG (page number) *A Letter from a Gentleman to His Friend in Edinburgh*, edited by Ernest C. Mossner and John V. Price (Edinburgh: Edinburgh University Press, 1967)

NHR (part. paragraph) *The Natural History of Religion*, edited by H. E. Root (Stanford: Stanford University Press, 1956).

NL (letter number. page) *New Letters of David Hume*, edited by Raymond Klibansky and Ernest C. Mossner (Oxford: Clarendon Press, 1954).

T (book. part. section. paragraph) *A Treatise of Human Nature*, edited by David Fate Norton and Mary J. Norton (Oxford: Oxford University Press, 2000).

Chapter 1

The Conventional Story of Hume on God

Hume's Reputation

It is part of the received history of Western civilization that David Hume, the famous Scottish philosopher and historian, is an avowed opponent of all things religious. He is a dismantler of theistic proofs, a disbeliever in the life to come and miracles, and a railer against all forms of religious practices, like prayer and worship. But above all, Hume is reputed to be a champion of secularism and skepticism, since he has conclusively shown that belief in God is a vestige from an earlier, unsophisticated age. Abundant evidence of this reputation can be found in the popular histories and surveys of intellectualism.

> Whenever the subject of 'natural religion' arises in his writings, Hume makes no secret of his view that he does not believe religion to have any rational foundations at all. . . . What Hume had done was remove any philosophical *necessity* for believing in God. Being himself a sunny, cheerfully-disposed individual, he appears to have felt no particular sorrow that we live in an empty, Godless universe, devoid of purpose.[1]

In her celebrated history, *Doubt,* Jennifer Michael Hecht offers this judgment of Hume's position on the divine:

> It is difficult to say whether Hume believed in God. In the penultimate chapter of his *Enquiry into Human Understanding* (1748), he has a character take up the role of defender of the tenets of Epicurus, which deny 'a divine existence and consequently a providence and a future state.' In this way Hume presented many arguments against contemporary believers but exclaimed 'O Athenians!' every once in a while to remind readers that he was really just talking to the ancient Greeks. It reads remarkably like a man finished with God, not least because he talks about how useless the concept became once we had agreed that we could not know anything about him.[2]

Certainly, there is an element of truth in these assertions. Hume was definitely skeptical about many things. He wrote an essay against the possibility of miracles, he rejected the 'superstitions' and 'enthusiasms' of the religious groups of modern Europe, he argued against the need for a religious basis to morality, and he subjected the teleological argument for the existence of God to one of its most searching investigations. In short, he found much in religion to which he objected. However, the quotations cited above paint Hume in a different hue than the one that emerges from a close reading of his actual writings. Hume, as will be shown, was not finished with God, nor did he think we live in a godless universe. He did not view all religious conclusions as irrational. In particular, there are many places where he notes that intellectual reflections yield the conclusion that there is a divine being. My aim is to provide a corrective for the determination – rampant through both scholarly and popular literature – that Hume has shown that belief in God is silly, irrational and without any intellectual justification at all.

This book will unfold in the following manner. The first chapter will take a snapshot of current thinking regarding Hume's conclusions about God, a state of affairs that I call the *conventional story*. Chapter 2 focuses on an under-studied, but often-cited, aspect of Hume's literary style – his use of irony. The relationship between Hume's philosophy of religion and deism will be explored in Chapter 3. The last two chapters will be devoted to exploring Hume's 'genuine theism'. The fourth chapter will provide textual support for the conclusion that Hume did believe in a divine being, and the fifth chapter will discuss the attributes of that deity.

The Conventional Story

One of the primary concerns of the 18th century British intellectuals was the possibility of *natural theology*, namely, the project of discovering theological truths about the nature and existence of God through an examination of the physical world. Important works like John Locke's *The Reasonableness of Christianity* (1695) defended the intellectual integrity of the doctrines and beliefs of the Christian religion, while the Boyle Lectures of Samuel Clarke in 1704 and 1705 rose to meet the challenges of a new age and to assert the certainty of philosophical arguments for God and the possibility of an intellectual defense of Christianity. The titles of Clarke's published lectures reveal these purposes: *A Demonstration of the Being and Attributes of God* (1704) and *A Discourse concerning the Unchangeable Obligations of Natural Religion, and the Truth and Certainty of the Christian Revelation* (1705).

The project of natural theology was taken up by another group of thinkers, known as *Deists*, with a more radical agenda than a philosophical defense of Christianity. The deists raised serious questions about the plausibility of divine revelation and insisted instead on a religion whose doctrines were formed solely on the basis of reason and natural theology. Deism was not a uniform movement, but, rather, a sprawling, multi-pronged effort which defies easy definition. The flood of books that announced the deist movement included these prominent offerings: John Toland's *Christianity not Mysterious* (1696), Anthony Collins' *Discourse on Free-Thinking* (1713) and Matthew Tindal's *Christianity as Old as the Creation* (1730). The popularity of deism provoked responses from several more orthodox thinkers, including the important critiques of Joseph Butler (*Analogy of Religion*, 1736) and George Berkeley (*Alciphron*, 1732).

It is in the context of these debates that David Hume (born in 1711) came to intellectual maturity. Even on his deathbed in 1776, he recalled for James Boswell that while he had read Clarke and Locke in his youth, he was not persuaded by their arguments.[3] Despite this disavowal, it is clear that Hume was thoroughly immersed in the philosophical questions that emerged from the natural religion debates, given that he wrote more about religion (save history) than on any other topic.[4] Among the questions that interested Hume were the arguments for the existence of God, the possibility of miracles, the role of God in the world, the origins of religions, the origin of religious belief and the effect of religion on ethics.

David Hume was born on 26 April 1711 in Edinburgh, Scotland to a good family with little money. Hume's father, John Home (Hume changed the spelling of his last name to match its pronunciation), died when David was only 2 years old. His mother, Katherine, raised David and his older brother and sister in their country home in Ninewells. Hume proved to have a prodigious intellect which his family hoped would lead him into the practice of law, but Hume found himself more comfortable in the world of letters and thought. Indeed, he conceded in a short autobiography ('My Own Life') written at the end of his life that his ruling passion was 'my Love of literary Fame'.[5]

Ironically, Hume was much better known in his own day as an essayist and historian than as a philosopher. His first book, *A Treatise of Human Nature* 'fell *dead-born from the Press,* without reaching such distinction as even to excite a Murmur among the Zealots', to quote Hume's famous assessment. He achieved the much-desired notoriety and fortune from his literary essays and the multi-volume *History of England*. He became the toast of France and enjoyed the company of leading *philosophes* like Denis Diderot and Baron d'Holbach. He corresponded with intellectual leaders like Benjamin Franklin, Adam Smith and Voltaire and endured a painful extended visit from the unstable Jean-Jacques Rousseau. Immanuel Kant credited Hume with awakening him from his 'dogmatic slumbers', thus enabling him to produce the works of his 'critical' period.

Hume was a major player in the Enlightenment, yet it is a mistake to think of him simply in those terms. He was an eclectic thinker, one who found himself somewhat torn between the attraction of skepticism and the desire, endemic in all philosophers, to discover and express the truth. As he is more explicitly skeptical than most philosophers, it is natural to pay special attention to that aspect of his thought, but it is, nevertheless, a faux pas to reduce him to a metaphysical and religious dismantler. Hume found himself in the midst of a swirl of intellectual trends. The rising Enlightenment mentality challenged religious dogmatism and superstition, replacing it with scientific experimentation and empirical thought. Hume was, of course, very attracted to this way of thinking. However, he had a great deal of respect for religious thinkers like Hutcheson and Butler, and many of his closest friends were well-educated clergy in Edinburgh. Though he found much in religion that he despised and rejected, he did not repudiate the entire enterprise in the ways that children of the Enlightenment, like Nietzsche and Freud, would do. Instead, Hume carved out a unique niche for himself – a set of religious beliefs and positions, and the justification of them – that was not found in any thinkers that predated him.

However, this interest, even obsession, with religious issues is not generally reflected in the Hume scholarship of the last 100 years. The history of the interpretation of Hume in the 20th century has several important turning points. It is generally acknowledged by Hume scholars that the work of Norman Kemp Smith in the 1940s opened the door for a much more complete understanding of Hume than had ever existed before. Prior to Kemp Smith, Hume was viewed primarily as a destructive skeptic or a forerunner of the logical positivists. The era that followed Kemp Smith made great strides in overcoming these caricatures of Hume's thought, but still tended to see Hume solely through Book 1 of the *Treatise*, thus focusing primarily on his epistemology at the expense of other aspects of Hume's thought. For instance, Kemp Smith's book, *The Philosophy of David Hume*, does not have a single chapter on Hume's philosophy of religion.[6] This narrow focus has given rise to the conventional story of Hume on religion and God.

Since the mid-1980s, however, a broader picture has begun to emerge with the work of Hume scholars like David Fate Norton, Donald Livingston and Claudia Schmidt who have specifically sought to articulate a comprehensive picture of Hume, using all his works and encompassing all the philosophical issues to which he devoted his energies. Despite these advances, however, several of the mistakes and omissions of the Kemp Smith era still need to be addressed, especially regarding his theism.

This conventional story regarding Hume and religion often has a systemic (as opposed to textual) starting point. For example, the interpreter may begin with Hume's empiricism and describe Hume as holding that the only legitimate knowledge claims are those which arise from impressions of sensations. This perspective, of course, arises out of Book 1 of the *Treatise*, and naturally leads to this question – but what sensations do we have of God or of the truths of religion? Since there are no sensations, there can be no true knowledge of anything transcendent, thus no religious beliefs are justified. This way of thinking is the track that the logical positivists followed.

The conventional story could also be told from the starting point of skepticism. For instance, the skeptical Hume, appearing in the guise of Philo in the *Dialogues concerning Natural Religion*, uncovers the many problems and difficulties in the argument from design, and thus undercuts responsible belief in the existence of God. Or, again, the skeptical Hume shows his disdain for the possibility of miracles in the famous section from *An Enquiry concerning Human Understanding*. Added to these pessimistic conclusions is an ample selection of Hume's many disparaging comments on the effect of religion on morals and society, condemnations of the fanatics and the enthusiasts, and other generally critical comments on religion and deity which putatively call forth the conclusion that Hume is universally dismissive of all things having to do with religion. One passage from *The Natural History of Religion* will suffice as an example of Hume's frequent criticisms of popular religion:

> Nay, if we should suppose, what never happens, that a popular religion were found, in which it was expressly declared, that nothing but morality could gain the divine favour; if an order of priests were instituted to inculcate this opinion, in daily sermons, and with all the arts of persuasion; yet so inveterate are the people's prejudices, that, for want of some other superstition, they would make the very attendance on these sermons the essentials of religion, rather than place them in virtue and good morals. (NHR 14.3)[7]

The question to be asked, however, is whether disparaging comments like these are indicative of an entirely negative and dismissive judgment by

Hume against all religious beliefs and conclusions. In actuality, the texts of Hume tell a different story.

The last part of the conventional story is that Hume is judged to be an opponent of theism. This quotation from A. J. Ayer serves to illustrate the tenor of this aspect of the conventional story:

> [Hume] was, as I have tried to show, campaigning on many fronts against religious belief, but above all he wished to preserve philosophy from the 'license of fancy and hypothesis' into which theology falls. We have seen that he was not a model of consistency, but he was at least consistent in his naturalism, his insistence that every branch of science be anchored in experience.[8]

Typical also is the conclusion of John Valdimir Price, who writes that 'we know that Hume himself unreservedly held nontheistic positions [at least in part because]. . . if the existence of God can be doubted for any consider-able time, then it is an existence whose evidence is not enough to convince an empiricist.'[9]

The Puzzlement Factor and Affirmation Texts

The account given thus far of the conventional story is not complete, how-ever, because all thorough attempts to explain Hume's conclusion regarding God must include what I call the *puzzlement factor*. The puzzlement factor arises because those who adhere to the conventional story are perplexed by the presence throughout Hume's writings of expressions of belief in the existence of a deity. For instance, Hume's *Natural History* contains this passage in the preface:

> As every inquiry, which regards religion, is of the utmost importance, there are two questions in particular, which challenge our attention, to wit, that concerning its foundation in reason, and that concerning its origin in human nature. Happily, the first question, which is the most important, admits of the most obvious, at least, the clearest, solution. The whole frame of nature bespeaks an intelligent author; and no rational enquirer can, after serious reflection, suspend his belief a moment with regard to the primary principles of genuine Theism and Religion. (NHR Introduction)

Also, there is the famous reversal of Philo in the *Dialogues*, who, after repeated skeptical jibes targeted at arguments for the existence of God, affirms his belief in the deity in Part 12. Earlier, however, Philo had the following to say on the question of the deity:

> But surely, where reasonable men treat these subjects, the question can never be concerning the *being*, but only the *nature* of the Deity. The former truth, as you well observe, is unquestionable and self-evident. Nothing exists without a cause; and the original cause of the universe (whatever it be) we call God; and piously ascribe to him every species of perfection. (DNR 2.3)

Some commentators, like Price, attribute deity-affirming texts like this one to irony. 'What would appear as professions of faith in the *Dialogues*, then, are not concessions to the pious; loaded with ambiguity, they are instead ironic counterthrusts to those who demand uniform faith and piety from all.'[10] Others, like Terence Penelhum, are genuinely puzzled and truly wrestle with the implications of these texts:

> So I think that Hume is attacking what was part of the conventional wisdom of his own day: the assumption that the propositions of deism can be inferred by any rational man from the observation of the natural order. Far less than this can be inferred. But again, Hume is far from crystal clear whether he thinks that *none* of it can. On the balance I think that his position is not wholly negative [that is, atheistic], as Kemp Smith suggests, but that he does grudgingly come to accept *some* part of the deistic position, at least as much which is contained in the proposition, 'That the cause or causes of order in the universe probably bear some remote analogy to human intelligence'. How positive this is I am not at all sure.[11]

The point here is that there are within the Humean corpus many texts which, on their face, seem to run counter to the conventional story. These passages (which I will call *affirmation texts*) make the interpretation of what Hume actually believed with regard to the existence and nature of God a significant and challenging venture. It is my contention that the conventional story is an inaccurate picture of Hume's true beliefs regarding God, and that it needs to be replaced with an interpretation that takes more seriously these deity-affirming texts. In other words, what is needed is a reading of Hume on the nature and existence of God that is driven more by the *texts* of Hume, rather than systemic concerns. It is not Hume's skepticism alone nor his empiricism by itself that will ultimately answer this question, but rather a close reading of what he actually wrote, that will yield the proper guidance with regard to this enquiry.

In order, then, to render an accurate accounting of Hume's theism, a thorough review of his writings, published and unpublished, is necessary. Explicitly stated, the question I will answer is *what exactly did Hume himself conclude regarding the existence of God.* Closely related to this question is the query regarding the nature of the deity. *If there is a god,*[12] *then what is this being like?* I will weigh all the relevant textual evidence, consider the significant contextual and hermeneutical issues, and finally argue for a reading of Hume's conclusions regarding the existence and nature of God that is more accurate and sophisticated than the conventional story. It is worth noting that while there is substantial interaction with the secondary literature on Hume, my primary goal is not to refute point by point all commentators whose interpretation differs from mine. Rather, I will take a textual approach and offer a fresh reading of the relevant texts in an effort to uncover what Hume genuinely thought about the deity.

A prudent beginning is to review the two main ways in which Hume's conclusions regarding God have been interpreted according to the conventional story. The first way is to see Hume as an *atheist* or *agnostic.* I will consider the commentary offered by Antony Flew as representative of this approach. The other main interpretive move is best exemplified by J. C. A. Gaskin, who sees Hume as a deist, specifically – to use Gaskin's celebrated phrase – as an *attenuated deist.*

Hume as an Atheist/Agnostic:
Antony Flew

Historically, the most common approach to Hume's philosophy of religion is to see him as an atheist or an agnostic. Since atheism (the active denial of the existence of a deity) is a bolder claim in general and since Hume never refers to himself as an atheist, students of Hume are more likely to peg him as an agnostic, that is, one who remains skeptical of metaphysical claims (pro or con) regarding the existence of a divine being. The two positions have more in common, however, than they have differences, and so it is convenient to consider them together, remembering, of course, that the terms are not synonymous. No doubt, the standard-bearer for this approach is Antony Flew,[13] who has been writing on Hume throughout most of the second half of the twentieth century and into the next. Flew's summary judgment on Hume's conclusions regarding the existence and nature of

God is categorically stated in the Introduction to his edited volume on Hume's *Writings on Religion*. It is worth quoting at length:

David Hume (1711–1776) was a complete unbeliever, the first major thinker of the modern period to be through and through secular, this-worldly, and man-centered. He was always too prudent, too tactful in his concern to preserve smooth relations with his many friends among the Moderate faction of the Scottish clergy, and too much of the principled sceptic, ever to proclaim himself an atheist. . . . The most, however, that Hume was prepared positively to affirm was the bare existence of a Deity, about the essential nature of which nothing whatever can be known; and which could, surely, not be identified as an entity separate and distinct from the Universe itself. The '*true* religion', to which Hume professed his devotion, was persuasively defined to exclude all actual religious belief and practice. For he made no bones about his disbeliefs in both human immortality and any kind of Divine interventions, miraculous or otherwise, in the ordinary course of nature.[14]

Though it will be necessary to explore many of these assertions, little analysis is needed to observe an incoherence already present in just this passage. One is hard pressed to understand how Hume can be a 'complete unbeliever' and one who is 'thorough[ly] secular, this-worldly and man-centered' and still be one who affirms the existence of a Divine Being! This tension reflects the puzzlement element in the conventional story, but it also foreshadows the systemic failure of Flew to accurately describe what Hume has concluded regarding the nature and existence of God.

The story that Flew tells of Hume's atheism contains three distinct acts: the presumption of atheism, Flew's categorizations of Hume's position on God and the religious hypothesis. To begin, Flew argues that the appropriate initial attitude an individual should bring to an investigation of the existence of God is a 'presumption of atheism', which is 'closely analogous to the presumption of innocence in the English law'. In other words, for Flew, the onus of proof in this discussion falls on the theist. The proper intellectual default position is that one should assume that there is no divine being, until one is shown to exist.[15] As Flew contends in an essay entitled 'The Presumption of Atheism', the burden falls on the one asserting the proposition *a god exists* to show that the denial of the proposition *a god does not exist* is wrong. The analogy is again to a criminal trial in which the prosecution needs to show the defendant guilty beyond reasonable doubt in order to overcome the initial presumption of innocence.[16]

Two points are in order at this juncture. First, it seems to me that the analogy between the two presumptions is a false one. The defendant is presumed innocent in order that his or her human rights may be protected. It is a measure of respect accorded to human individuals in order to ensure that the deprivation of liberty and freedom that will result from a conviction is not taken unjustifiably. However, in the realm of ideas and debate, it is not necessary to offer propositions and positions the same sort of respect. A proposition cannot be unjustly imprisoned, so the basis for the analogy is shown to be false.

In addition, with regard to an accused individual, it is the case that he/she is either guilty or innocent, and that the closest thing to a neutral position at the beginning of an examination of the accused is the presumption of innocence. Similarly, a proposition is either true or false. However, it is not clear that the neutral position regarding a proposition is to deny it, especially since a debate, by definition, involves opposing propositions. In the deliberation over the existence of the deity, for example, the propositions *a god exists* and *a god does not exist* are both claims about the true state of affairs in our universe. The truly neutral position is to withhold assent or dissent from both claims, not just one of them. The onus of proof or demonstration rests equally on both parties in a philosophical dispute and continues to rest on both of them to press their case until one party acquiesces or capitulates. To hold that the responsibility of proof rests only on the one asserting is to misunderstand in a rather serious way the nature of philosophical debate.

Second, the error of this assertion is significant, because Flew believes that Hume makes just such a presumption of atheism, 'The present presumption was apparently first clearly formulated as such by Strato, next but one in succession to Aristotle as head of the Lyceum. . . . It was this "Stratonician atheism" which was received by the young Hume as an emancipating revelation.'[17] The only support that Flew provides for this claim is a general reference to Hume's *Dialogues*, despite the fact that none of the interlocutors in those dialogues takes atheism as his starting point or refers to Strato. One also wonders how the 'young Hume' could have presumed atheism if it is something that came to him as an 'emancipating revelation'. He may have come to accept this position at some point in his intellectual development – whether he did is one of the main questions of this project – but it is unclear how Hume, raised in a Calvinist family in a predominantly Christian country, could have begun as an atheist.

Perhaps what Flew intended was not that Hume himself presumed atheism, but that he thought that one *should* presume atheism as an intellectual starting point. However, if this is indeed what Hume thought, it is certainly strange that none of the principals in the *Dialogues* endorses such a position, and that Hume never advocates such a point of view in any of his other writings. In fact, one of Hume's favorite quotations (from Francis Bacon) seemingly reflects just the opposite point of view. '*A little philosophy*, says lord Bacon, *makes men atheists: A great deal reconciles them to religion*' (NHR 6.2; see also DNR 1.18). Thus, it is clear that the presumption of atheism is not only illegitimate on its face, but also dubiously ascribed to Hume.

The second part of Flew's story of Hume's atheism is revealed by observing his different categorizations of Hume on this subject. There are four such descriptors in Flew's corpus, and a review of these categorizations pulls together his most important arguments for seeing Hume as a non-believer in God. The first is Hume as an *agnostic*, or, more specifically in Flew's terminology, an *aggressive agnostic*. From Flew's perspective, the word *agnostic* is usually used incorrectly to refer to an alternative, middle position between theism and atheism. Agnosticism, according to Flew, is not skepticism with regard to the possibility of knowing whether or not there is a god.[18] Flew aligns himself with T. H. Huxley and W. K. Clifford and proposes that the true understanding of agnosticism is as a methodological stance which provides one with guidance regarding when to assent to believe a notion. Clifford is famous for asserting that it is 'wrong always, everywhere, and for anyone, to believe anything upon insufficient evidence.'[19] Hume likewise is famous for asserting that 'A wise man proportions his belief to the evidence,' a notion that Flew names the *Agnostic Principle.*[20]

This notion of agnosticism is surely not in keeping with usual usage, which describes it as a kind of skepticism directed specifically at religion or the existence of God. Nevertheless, despite Flew's attempt to revise the sense of the word, in the end, he holds that the Agnostic Principle leads Hume to conclusions that are generally held to be agnostic in the typical sense of the word and which amount to a kind of practical atheism. Flew concludes that Hume's examinations of religion in his various writings have undermined the putatively rational foundations of both natural and revealed religion, and have demonstrated the impossibility of proving a miracle to be a possible foundation of a religious system.[21] Elsewhere, Flew concludes the matter in this way:

> In order to fulfill this corollary purpose [to provide a restraint against religious fears and prejudices] Hume had to justify an aggressive agnosticism: not just a feeble confession of individual unknowing; but instead a strong claim that positive knowledge must be, in this area, impossible.[22]

A second label that Flew proposes for Hume is *skeptical metaphysician.* Flew writes in his companion to the first *Enquiry* that, 'As a metaphysician, he is thoroughly skeptical.'[23] The specific context of this quotation refers to the notion of a soul, but Flew makes it clear that he sees the skepticism of Hume extending to the notion of the deity, in keeping with the assertions of the conventional story, in which Flew has great confidence. Things like matter, the soul, special creation and the god of the philosophers are all so removed from our experience that to assert the existence of such things (as Flew reads Hume) is the very opposite of scientific inquiry. None of these things can be studied scientifically, so the existence and nature of them remain hidden from us. The only possible stance is skepticism that does not just pull back from intellectual investigation, but precludes any such possibility.[24]

Flew, however, is not content simply to characterize Hume as an aggressive agnostic and a skeptic. He links Hume on a number of occasions with *Stratonician atheism,*[25] a term that has been noted already. This type of atheism refers specifically to the notion that 'since everything we observe in this world can be fully accounted for by other causes', there is no need to infer a god.[26] Stratonician atheism, then, is the naturalistic point of view that since God is not necessary to explain the world, there is no god.

In one of his most direct comments on Hume's theological beliefs, Flew offers this assessment:

> Since the *Dialogues* are indeed dialogues, very scrupulously composed on the model particularly of Cicero's *de Natura Deorum,* it is no more possible to deduce Hume's personal position directly from this text than we can deduce Shakespeare's political and religious convictions from his plays. But in Hume's case we have sufficient biographical evidence for it to be a tolerably safe bet that it was what, following Bayle, Hume called Stratonician atheism. If this conjecture is correct, then the final conviction of the author of the *Dialogues* was that we have to accept as ultimate the existence of the Universe and the subsistence of whatever our scientists find to be its fundamental laws.[27]

This quotation is worthy of comment on several fronts. First, Flew provides none of the biographical evidence to which he alludes (nor does he offer any citation where it may be found), and which leads him to conclude that it is a 'tolerably safe bet' that Hume is an atheist. Secondly, it is rather astounding that Flew holds in this passage that it is impossible to determine what Hume thinks about God from the *Dialogues,* since in many other places, he (and scores of other Hume scholars) attempts to do just this very thing! Both of these points will be examined in due course, but it is important in this context to note that Flew has identified Hume with Stratonician atheism in several places, suggesting that for Hume, the debate on the existence of God has been concluded and that the negative answer has prevailed.

Finally, Flew holds that Hume is 'through and through secular, this-worldly and man-centred'.[28] What is important about this categorization is the context in which Flew offers it. It is in a section of *Hume's Philosophy of Belief* in which Flew is countering a claim by G. J. Warnock that Hume's thought is relevant for 'morality perhaps but on religion not at all'.[29] Flew (rightly) objects to this conclusion on the basis of it being made presumably only with the *Treatise* in mind. What Flew believes is that Hume has made serious contributions to religion, and among them is the notion that one ought to be thoroughly secular, this-worldly and human-oriented. There is no rational reason for any supernatural or spiritual reflections or investigations. According to Flew, those sorts of things are ruled out by Hume, and this insight is Hume's rather damning contribution to religion. A closer reading of Hume will show, however, that he does not abjure religion and God, but rather his attempt is to investigate to what degree experimental reasoning sheds any light on these topics. Even in the famous essay on miracles, Hume's agenda is to consider what sorts of evidence would have to be in place in order for one to legitimately believe that a miracle had occurred. For Hume, it is a question of evidence and arguments, not an attempt to rule these sorts of topics off-limits or out-of-bounds.

There are, therefore, good reasons to reject all of Flew's labels and the conclusions that stand behind them. The puzzlement factor alone is enough to question whether Hume is rightly seen as an agnostic or an atheist, and the affirmation texts preclude Hume from being the kind of this-worldly secularist Flew describes him to be. Interestingly, Flew himself occasionally reflects some doubts about these classifications, as is evident in this passage:

> He [Hume] believed, too, that it was precisely the uninterrupted order of nature which constituted the chief, if not the only, ground for even that completely empty and nominal theism which was the maximum in the way of religious dogma to which as a philosopher he was able to give his rational assent.[30]

This passage betrays a greater concession of religious belief on the part of Hume than Flew was otherwise willing to give in his four classifications, and it appears that Flew attempts to mitigate this inconsistency by excessive qualification. Nevertheless, Hume's repeated assertions of God's existence force Flew to acknowledge them, even if they run counter to the conclusions already offered. It is hard to see how Hume could be an aggressive agnostic, a Stratonician atheist, thoroughly secular and a complete unbeliever and still admit to any kind of theism, even one as exhaustively qualified as the position outlined above.

The last act of Flew's story arises out of Sections 10 and 11 of the first *Enquiry* which delineate Hume's *religious hypothesis* (also known as the argument from design):

> What Hume mischievously christens 'the religious hypothesis' is the assumption that this argument establishes the existence of a God with characteristics from which conclusions of human interest, which could not be known by direct inspection of the Universe around us, could be validly inferred. Or, at least, that it establishes the existence of an intervening God and one who might reasonably be expected to be going to reveal, or to have revealed, facts of supreme human interest. And what could be of greater human interest than the news that we are all going to enjoy eternal bliss or suffer eternal torture?[31]

That Hume raises significant questions about the design argument (in both Section 11 and also in the *Dialogues*) is not a matter of dispute. Flew summarizes Hume's argument in Section 11 as being composed of two broad points. First, since the cause (God) is known only by the effects (the universe), then one cannot predicate anything of the cause beyond what is known by the effects. The argument from design cannot lead to conclusions about God's goodness or omniscience, so those attributes cannot be ascribed to the being who is the conclusion of this argument.[32] The second point arises from the following consideration. When you see a half-finished building, do you not expect that it is the work of some builder? Or when you see a footprint, do you not look for another? In other words, do not the evidences of design indicate at least something about a designer, if nothing else than just the brute fact that there is one? (EHU 11.1.24). The skeptical answer is that the similarity between 'human art and contrivance' and the work of the deity is not suitable for constructing an analogy, due, at least in part, to the fact that the universe and the deity are unique objects (EHU 11.1.25–27). Thus, any analogous reasoning based on them leads to hasty generalizations:

Flew interprets Section 10 ('Of Miracles') of the first *Enquiry* as working together with Section 11 to form a larger assault on the project of natural reason as a whole:

> The former tries to show that there cannot be evidence sufficient by itself to prove the occurrence of miracles, so as to authenticate a religious

revelation. The latter attempts to establish that we cannot call up reserves of support from any systems of natural theology, to give the occurrence of some miraculously endorsed revelation any antecedent probability. Although Hume was for good reason unwilling ostentatiously to underline the point of Section XI he did say enough to leave the careful reader in no doubt that he himself appreciated that the main argument of the earlier was dependent on the conclusion of the main argument of the later of these two Sections.[33]

Undoubtedly, Flew is right that these two sections do comprise an important two-pronged challenge for the whole project of natural theology. However, further discussion of this issue and a full response to Flew's assertions must be delayed until Chapters 4 and 5 when a more complete interpretation of Hume's corpus can be undertaken. At this point, however, one can see that Flew's characterization of Hume as an atheist/agnostic is too bold in light of the numerous affirmation texts. A more moderate position, and one that is more prevalent among Hume scholars, is to term Hume a deist. It is to that thesis that I now turn.

Hume as Deist: J. C. A. Gaskin

Perhaps the most respected commentator regarding Hume's thoughts on religion is J. C. A. Gaskin, whose *Hume's Philosophy of Religion* is widely considered the standard work on the topic. Gaskin introduces this work by observing that Hume was very much preoccupied with religious topics and issues, and that his treatment of these topics is negative, critical and destructive.[34] Gaskin holds that Hume's writings effectively undermine the project of natural religion, reveal some of the problems with the credentials of revelation and show that religion can actually have an adverse effect on morality. Finally, Gaskin interprets Hume as believing that religious beliefs arise from natural propensities which are not rational in nature.[35] These censures, Gaskin concludes, have a negative effect on Hume's theism:

> I shall try to show that Hume's critique as a whole moves steadily towards a consistent position which is short of atheism but has chilling consequences for personal religion. This position is that a vestigial design argument establishes a weak probability that natural order originates in the activity of something with intelligence remotely analogous to our own. This feeble *rational* datum is united with an insistent *feeling* in most

of us that natural order springs from a designer. When our philosophical assent to the existence of this designer has been given (that is to say our assent qualified by the exercise of mitigated scepticism) we recognise that it has no moral claim on us, nor we upon it. I call this position 'attenuated deism'.[36]

It is immediately clear that Gaskin's interpretation of Hume on the existence and nature of God avoids some of the mistakes which characterize Flew's point of view. For one, Gaskin recognized that Hume's position falls 'short of atheism'. Also, Gaskin discusses the notion of *natural belief*, a concept which helps to make clear some of the nuances of Hume's reflections on the phenomena of religious belief, although the phrase itself is not Hume's.[37] Certainly, however, the most distinctive aspect of Gaskin's interpretation of Hume on the existence and nature of the deity is his proposal that Hume's position is an *attenuated deism*. It will be shown in due course that both Gaskin's position on this question is incomplete and his name for it imprecise. In this chapter, however, I will sketch out what Gaskin sees as the structure of Hume's critique of religion and natural theology, and discuss his proposal that Hume is an attenuated deist. A full critique of Gaskin will not be accomplished until the investigation of the relationship of Hume to 18th century deism is offered in Chapter 3.

According to Gaskin, Hume's philosophy of religion reaches these negative conclusions: (1) Religious metaphysics is beyond our understanding because of the mitigated skepticism which Hume advocates. (2) It is necessary to separate religion and morality, due to the superstitions and enthusiasms of religion. (3) There are no empirical grounds for the belief that there is a self or an immortal soul, so the hope of an afterlife is a futile one. (4) Finally, there are the exposés of religious fanaticism and superstition in the *History of England* and the naturalistic evaluation of the origins and character of religions offered in the *Natural History*.[38] While only the first of these conclusions is directly related to the question of Hume's beliefs concerning the deity, all are important for underscoring how complete and destructive Gaskin sees Hume's evaluation of religion.

There is some reason to think that Gaskin is unduly negative in his assessment of Hume on religion. For instance, Donald Livingston has argued extensively that Hume's real agenda is to distinguish between true religion and false religion.[39] Livingston claims that for Hume, true religion is a species of true philosophy and false religion grows out of false philosophy. Religion and philosophy grow out of original propensities that exist in human beings, but true religion (*philosophical theism*) develops when mankind stops living in fear of the gods of polytheism and embraces the wonder of a world ordered by a single deity:

> Philosophical theism is the most developed form of causal reasoning, and the belief that the universe is a system which is the result of purposive intelligence is a belief constitutive of the scientific community. It is because of his own adherence to philosophical theism that Hume could scandalize the polite atheists at Holbach's dinner party by insisting that he had never met a true atheist.[40]

Clearly, there is more to be said here regarding these vastly different conceptions of Hume's religious beliefs, but this discussion will be reprised when I offer my reading of the *Natural History* and the *Dialogues*.

The most critical aspect of Gaskin's analysis of Hume is his assessment that Hume is an attenuated deist.[41] For Gaskin, this position is a middle ground between the extremes of atheism and theism but one which does not simply mean some sort of agnosticism. Gaskin disagrees with Flew and explicitly affirms that Hume was not an atheist. He articulates a difference between an *absolute atheist* and a *relative atheist*, the former being the individual who explicitly denies the existence of any sort of divine being, while the latter is 'one who believes in a more contracted or radically different idea of god from that which prevails in their society.'[42] Hume was not, according to Gaskin, an absolute atheist.

> Again and again in private and published work Hume gives explicit or implicit assent to the proposition *that there is a god*. This assent is elicited by the recognition that the order to be found in nature *could* (not must) be explained as the work of an ordering agent.[43]

The use of the phrase *relative atheist* is applied to certain 18th century thinkers, like Anthony Collins and Matthew Tindal, whose unconventional views regarding God or divine revelation usually resulted in the accusation of atheism or deism. Thus, the term is more a term of abuse (as Gaskin acknowledges) than a helpful term for sorting out divergent theological views. Even so, Gaskin leaves open the possibility that Hume could be a relative atheist (as Gaskin defines the term).[44] But certainly, this ambiguity is misleading, since using the word *atheism* runs contrary to Gaskin's assertion that Hume does endorse some version of theism. I find the distinction between absolute and relative atheist to be vacuous and unhelpful. Better descriptions can be found for those whose positions fall short of a complete denial of a god but also do not endorse the god of a specific religion.

By naming Hume an *attenuated deist*, Gaskin hopes to capture the notion that Hume agrees with one of the conclusions of the deists, namely, that there is a god, but not, contrary to most deists, on the basis of any proofs of natural religion. Gaskin's clearest statement of what he means by this partial deism is the following passage. He believes that he has shown that Hume 'shares the implicit deistic rejection of revealed religion and agrees that there is a god, but one in relation to whom only cautious use of the words "intelligence" and "orderer" is possible.'[45] In addition, this deity, in virtue of his deficiencies and weaknesses, can have no moral hold on us.

This articulation of Hume's position on the deity is problematic in several ways. While it may be an improvement on Flew's position that Hume denied the existence of God, it addresses the nature of God in a superficial way, and it also fails to pay sufficient attention to the complicated path that Hume takes to arrive at this conclusion. Nor does it appreciate the complexity of his specific relationship with the argument from design. Gaskin rightly recognizes that Hume is not in complete agreement with the deists of his day on the question of God, but to simply suggest that Hume has shorn off some elements of a 'typically' deistic position is to grossly understate the complexity of the deist movement and Hume's theism.

Another significant problem with Gaskin's attenuated deism is that the designation is imprecise and misleading in a way similar to *relative atheism*. As I will show, Hume is not really a deist, and the notion of attenuated deism is not a precise enough phrase for capturing the essence of Hume's conclusions regarding the deity. Ironically, Gaskin is aware of some of these difficulties, since much of his article 'Hume's Attenuated Deism' is devoted to developing reasons why Hume should *not* be seen as a deist! The most important of these reasons is that Hume repeatedly disavowed the term, especially given that in the social context of Hume's day, the term *deist* was a term of approbation.[46] Gaskin, however, is unswayed:

> But I am not (yet) repentant [over the use of this designation]. I still think that the tag 'attenuated deism' is not only the best phrase with which to indicate Hume's view, but also that it is a phrase which well summarizes the most reasonable conclusion which a dispassionate investigation is likely to draw from the available evidence.[47]

There is, however, another reason to not name Hume a deist, one that Gaskin does not address. Very simply, it is that the use of the term *deism* (much like *postmodernism* in today's context) is varied, complex and inconsistent, with the result that there is no agreement regarding what exactly a deist is or was. In the 17th and 18th century, the term was used loosely and almost always in a negative or abusive manner. In our contemporary scene, deism usually refers to the single belief in a caretaker deity, one who created the world, but shows no inclination to interfere or participate in the affairs of the world.[48] But this notion is far removed from the worldviews of individuals like John Toland, Anthony Collins, Matthew Tindal and others who usually are considered to be deists, but were concerned about a complicated mix of issues including the possibility of revelation, the nature of God, the use of reason in theology, biblical interpretation, the nature of the Trinity, the possibility of natural theology and others. One specific reason why the notion of *attenuated deism* itself is of little help is that Samuel Clarke listed four different kinds of deism in his Boyle lectures of 1704 and 1705.[49] Of which kind of deism does Hume espouse an attenuated version? In what sense is it attenuated? What does this reveal about the kind of god that Hume acknowledges? None of these questions can be answered by Gaskin via the analysis that he has presented.

The fault does not lie only with Gaskin, however. In Hume scholarship as a whole, there has not been sufficient attention paid to Hume's relationship with the theological debates swirling around the deism controversy of the early part of the 18th century, despite the fact that one cannot truly understand what Hume is rejecting and accepting on the question of God without a grasp of the intellectual discussions of this era. This lacuna will hopefully be remedied, at least in part, by Chapter 3.

Another commentator who interprets Hume as espousing a weakened form of theism is Keith Yandell, who asserts in his book *Hume's 'Inexplicable Mystery'* that Hume holds to a 'diaphanous theism' on the basis of innate propensities which human beings possess. Yandell cites this passage from the end of the *Natural History*:

> The universal propensity to believe in invisible, intelligent power, if not an original instinct, being at least a general attendant of human nature, may be considered as a kind of mark or stamp, which the divine workman has set upon his work; and nothing surely can more dignify mankind, than to be thus selected from all other parts of the creation, and to bear the image or impression of the universal Creator. (NHR 15.5)

Yandell offers this interpretation of Hume on God:

> In these passages, Hume ascribes belief in invisible, intelligent power as cause of natural order to a propensity which he describes as 'universal'

but 'secondary'. It is efficacious – called into effect by experience of
natural order – in almost everyone. In some, it leads to polytheism, in
others to monotheism, in each case in a variety of formulations and
versions. It is clear that the so-called theism to which a secondary propensity is said to lead is a very *thin* theism. Omniscience, omnipotence and
omnibenevolence are not in view; neither is creation or providence. The
'power' is not Judge or Savior. No revelation, and no action in history, is
ascribed to this power. Morality is not based on appeal to this power's
nature or to its will. Even a deist deity who creates a world and leaves it
alone is religiously 'thicker' than the power this propensity posits. So the
use of 'theism' for the view in question is clearly challengeable, although
I shall retain it for sheer convenience.[50]

The point of highlighting Yandell's diaphanous theism (and Gaskin's
attenuated deism, for that matter) is to reveal how difficult it is to maintain
the conventional story while making sense of the affirmation texts. Gaskin
distorts the notion of deism and then erroneously attributes it to Hume,
while Yandell constructs a notion of divinity that is so strange that even
he admits it is questionably identified as a god. It is time for a reevaluation
of Hume on God, which jettisons the unnecessary baggage of the conventional story, in favor of a fresh reading of what Hume actually says about
the deity.

Chapter 2

Hume and Irony

Skepticism and Irony

Any attempt to correctly interpret David Hume's views on a particular topic must take into account two major, preliminary issues in order to avoid mis-interpretation. Interestingly, one of these issues (the problem of Hume's skepticism) is much discussed and rehearsed, while the other (the problem of Hume's use of irony) is frequently mentioned, but rarely investigated in any detail. On skepticism, I have nothing new to say, but that is not the case with Hume's use of irony.

That Hume was enamored of skepticism and spoke in favor of it on a number of occasions is not in doubt. The questions then are to what degree is he a skeptic and what is the nature of his skepticism. My judgment on these questions is that Hume refuses to embrace a totalizing skepti-cism, because, for him, skepticism is a methodology, not a set of skeptical conclusions. He calls this position *mitigated skepticism* (see EHU 12.2–3, cf. T 1.4.7.13–15), which is a middle ground between dogmatism and Pyrrhonism. Mitigated skepticism acts as a filter, and its function is to help distinguish between true and false philosophy. The implications of this kind of skepticism is that one should expect to find constructive philosophy in Hume (that is, positive philosophical assertions about the truth) as opposed to the wholesale negative critiques associated with complete skepticism. One would also expect from Hume evaluations regarding the relative strengths and weaknesses of the conclusions of his positive philosophy. This point is in keeping with his famous dictum that the wise man will propor-tion his belief to the evidence at hand (EHU 10.1.4).[1] Many examples of Hume distinguishing between true and false philosophy will be observed in the *Natural History* and *Dialogues*.

With regard to the second issue, it is somewhat ironic (pun intended) that, for all the attention paid to Hume's skepticism, the situation is wholly reversed with regard to the problem of irony. It is well recognized that Hume is an excellent writer, a master of the English language, and an individual who took great pains to carefully review and revise his writings throughout his life, even on his deathbed. In addition, it is often noted that Hume was a witty, jovial individual, who interjected this light-hearted aspect of his personality into his writings. Indeed, one commentator observed that the *Dialogues* are 'perhaps the funniest truly great work of philosophy ever written by anyone'.[2] The upshot is that many interpreters of Hume advise their readers to be aware of wit, sarcasm, irony and other similar literary devices that he is likely to employ in order that they not be hoodwinked into thinking that Hume always means exactly what he says. Certainly, this cautionary principle is correct. Hume does employ irony, and he is prone to write in dialogues which allow for the possibility that he can hide his true beliefs in a discussion which espouses many points of view.

What is unfortunately ignored by the majority of Hume scholars is that the task of identifying and interpreting these ironic or sarcastic utterances is not a self-evident, easy task, requiring little thought or reflection in order to do correctly.[3] The result is that Hume's use of irony is often appealed to, but rarely examined in a way that leads to some helpful hermeneutical principles which can uncover what Hume really intended to convey. This chapter will be aimed at exploring the nature of irony and developing these kinds of principles in order to determine when Hume did or did not intend irony. This project is especially important when the final goal is to determine what Hume concluded regarding a topic as controversial as the existence and nature of God.

A Lacuna Regarding Irony

Peter Millican offers this warning to readers of Hume, 'When reading Hume's writing on religion, it is important to remain alert to the possibility of irony in his apparent declarations of theistic belief.'[4] What is unfortunately missing from the large majority of these admonitions are instructions regarding how the reader is supposed to know when Hume is being ironic and when he is not. The most likely implication of this silence is that Hume scholars believe that it is rather a straightforward project to identify Hume's irony, despite the fact that they contend that one of Hume's purposes in using irony is to fool his Christian contemporaries into thinking that he is reiterating their beliefs, while cleverly intending just the opposite to his more sagacious readers.

> What would appear as professions of faith in the *Dialogues*, then, are not concessions to the pious; loaded with ambiguity, they are instead ironic counterthrusts to those who would demand uniform faith and piety from

all, under penalty of social obloquy or, sometimes, hanging. Hume would appear to yield to the demands of the pious and admit the existence of the sort of Deity in whom a belief was necessary. Faced with the prospect of making a living in a society whose views on religion were greatly at variance with his own, he had to be discreet and to mask his true feeling in irony; thus he deceived those who were stupid enough to be deceived. Working in this complex of social conditions, his irony had many functions.[5]

If Hume was able to fool his contemporaries with his subtle ironies – contemporaries, it must be noted, who shared the same culture, time and zeitgeist – it is a wonder, indeed, that the 21st century readers of Hume can so easily recognize his ironic statements without any need to investigate precisely what irony is, the purpose for its use, and (most importantly) how to recognize it when it appears.

By way of a convenient example of this scholarly neglect, one can consider the already-cited book that Millican edited on the first *Enquiry*. On four occasions,[6] the contributors note in passing Hume's use of irony with little or no argumentation to support the identification of irony in the instance at hand. It may, in fact, be the case that these scholars are ultimately justified in seeing irony in these instances, and it certainly cannot be expected that every identification of irony in Hume's writings be accompanied by a full discussion of the nature of irony. However, quick identifications of irony in Hume open up the possibility that Hume's texts will be interpreted according to the wishes of the interpreter rather than those of the author.

One of these four contributors, George Botterill, claims that the last paragraph of Section 8 ('On Liberty and Necessity') of the first *Enquiry* is 'a very masterpiece of ironic disingenuity' in which the 'camouflage is so flamboyantly disingenuous that we are left in no real doubt that Hume was more concerned that his real opinion on the subject should be discernible to the unprejudiced reader' than that he be judged by those whose opinion differed from his on the question of whether God is culpable as the mediate cause of the evil acts of human beings. Hume's discussion in this section neatly summarizes the intellectual difficulty faced by theists, who, on one hand, want to absolve God from being a cause of human evil, yet, on the other hand, wish not to affirm that mankind has complete liberty. Hume's concluding paragraph says, in essence, that this problem is an intractable mystery, and so it is necessary to focus on those intellectual problems that can be solved.

What I find problematic is not the perspective which sees Hume as being ironic, nor the intent to communicate this theological conundrum in a way which seems to make belief in a sovereign god a bit silly. Hume very well may intend just this reading. However, it is *also* possible to read Hume's text in the straightforward natural sense, namely, that this problem is truly one that is beyond human capacity to resolve. It is the failure to address this possible interpretation that I find objectionable. When this aspect of the analysis is absent, it then becomes too easy to make Hume say what the interpreter wants him to say. As a check then to potential bias in interpretation, the procedure for identifying irony in Hume needs to be specified.

This lack of attention to the nature of irony, and also to proper interpretive guidelines for identifying it, are particularly problematic when the interpreter of Hume turns to hotly debated passages like those associated with Philo's reversal in Part 12 of the *Dialogues*. Norman Kemp Smith advocates interpreting Philo as being duplicitous,[7] while Nelson Pike argues that Philo is voicing Hume's beliefs in Part 12.[8] A third position is offered by Terence Penelhum, who believes that the ironies in this section lie elsewhere.[9] However, in these long discussions by noted Hume scholars, what is lacking is a thorough discussion of what would be necessary in order to definitively interpret these passages as ironic or straightforward. The result is that opinion is stacked against opinion without clear resolution of what Hume intends, and the only thing that is certain is what the interpreters would say if they were to write a dialogue on natural religion!

It is certainly not my contention that Hume is never ironic. The capable reader who has read widely in Hume will readily recognize him as a clever writer, displaying wit, sarcasm, disdain and irony, among other literary talents. All contemporary accounts of Hume's personality affirm that he was a jovial individual who enjoyed a good joke and a company of people in which to tell it. It is, however, my conviction that in Hume's published works, it is sometimes very difficult to identify Hume's irony, and that, further, the common practice of simply asserting and identifying various passages as ironic without any supporting argumentation is, in fact, sloppy scholarship that is prone to error and bias. It is my intention in this chapter to fill in this scholarly lacuna by describing a procedure for interpreting Hume's irony.

Some Initial Distinctions

Some of the misunderstanding regarding Hume's irony can be set right with a proper understanding of what irony is and how it differs from related literary techniques. For instance, Ernest Mossner notes that *irony* is 'a figure of speech wherein the real meaning is concealed or contradicted by the words used.'[10] Mossner (who believes that Hume is to be solely identified with Philo in the *Dialogues*) goes on to remark that 'Hume ironically allows Cleanthes, rather than Philo, to refute Demea's *a priori* proof.'[11] The question to be asked, then, what exactly is the irony in this circumstance? According to the definition, irony is a *figure of speech*, but Mossner is not identifying a particular statement as ironic. What Mossner thinks is ironic is, in fact, the *circumstance* itself. If Philo is Hume's only spokesperson, one would expect that Philo would be the one to refute the rationalistic a priori proof that Demea offers. Proceeding, however, contrary to expectations, Hume uses Cleanthes to counter Demea. The irony then is in the unexpected juxtaposition of events, and not in the language itself.

This distinction is crucial, since the word *irony* is commonly used in these two senses. The first kind of irony refers to a state of affairs in which something unanticipated or contrary to expectations occurs. Examples include things like an accountant going bankrupt or a pastor who has an affair with another man's wife. The irony is in the unexpected quality of the circumstance, thus it can be called *circumstantial irony.*

A second kind of irony exists, however, that is closer to Mossner's definition. This type of irony is a literary device in which a person makes some statement P, but intends that her audience understand something different from P.[12] Often, this second kind of irony (*rhetorical irony*) is intended to be humorous or clever, since it implies some deeper level of interaction between the speaker/author and the audience. For instance, imagine two businesspeople are waiting together for a cab in cold, windy and rainy weather. If one of them says to the other, 'Beautiful day, isn't it?', the intention of the speaker is the exact opposite of what is said. The shared environment of the uncomfortable weather provides the necessary context for the listener to know that the natural sense of the statement is not the intended sense. If the same sentence had been exchanged by the same two businesspeople again waiting for a cab, but now on a sunny, clear day with temperature of 81°, it would clearly have not been rhetorical irony, but instead a statement intended to be taken at face value.

Neither Mossner nor John Price (author of *The Ironic Hume*, the only book-length treatment of Hume's irony) adequately address this distinction between circumstantial and rhetorical irony, which results in the kind of imprecise identification of irony that Mossner makes. Price magnifies the imprecision by naming no less than 11 different types of irony in Hume,[13] then neglects to catalog the various differences between these types of irony.

Circumstantial irony and rhetorical irony require distinct interpretive tasks. In the example cited from Mossner, one may ask in light of the fact that Cleanthes offers a Humean refutation to the a priori proof, whether Philo is indeed the only interlocutor that speaks for Hume. Maybe instead, Cleanthes is being set up for a different sort of response from Philo. Whatever the intent may have been, it is essential to note that the interpreter of circumstantial irony is *not* asking if the given proposition is supposed to be understood in some sense other than the natural sense, which is the interpretive question for rhetorical irony. Thus, failure to distinguish between these two senses of irony obscures the specifically different tasks of the interpreter in these two instances.

Several examples of the failure to perceive this distinction are found in *The Ironic Hume.* Hume enjoys highlighting instances of circumstantial irony (which Price calls *cosmic irony*) in the *History of England.* Price observes, 'By juxtaposing promises and actuality, aspirations and defeats, Hume, throughout the entire *History,* creates a cosmic irony that not only tries to restore events to their proper size but even wishes that contemporaries had been able to measure the truly important events.'[14] The example cited in this context by Price is that of Richard II, who, despite great potential for leadership, in fact, showed an absence of 'solid judgment' which resulted in numerous failures. (H 2.17.323–324) The problem is that Hume does not *create* this irony, as Price asserts. Rather, he is reporting the irony of the circumstances, which leaves for the reader the interpretative task of discerning why Hume mentions these circumstances.

Political partisans among Hume's contemporaries believed that they saw hidden agendas in Hume's telling of the history of England, despite Hume's repeated assertions that he was trying to be neutral and nonpartisan. It is possible that these assertions could be rhetorically ironic, and these are the kind of passages that are especially relevant and difficult, since they require the reader to invert the meaning of the passage. Price observes that 'Hume is both the writer of irony [rhetorical irony] . . . and the observer of irony in life [circumstantial irony].'[15] Yes, but what is neglected is that each type of irony presents its own set of interpretive requirements. To simply identify both instances as ironic does not do justice to the complexities of the texts and the different situations they represent.

Further ambiguities result from Price's failure to distinguish irony from sarcasm and wit in Hume's writings. Price cites a letter from Hume to his relative Lord Kames regarding an early draft of the essay on miracles, which included this request:

I beg of you to show it to no Body, except to Mr Hamilton, if he pleases; & let me know at your Leizure that you have receiv'd it, read it, & burnt it. I wou'd not even have you make another nameless Use of it, to which it wou'd not be improper, for fear of Accident. (NL 1.2)

Price argues at length that the reference to the 'nameless use' is ironic, since it reveals Hume's understanding of what those who support miracles would think of his essay and 'that the religionists would like nothing better than to make that "nameless Use" of his manuscript; if not, they would be likely to think that the reasoning in the essay was the intellectual equivalent of excrement and say so.'[16]

However, reading this text as ironic is to misunderstand what irony is. Hume's self-deprecating humor is very evident, and his modesty towards his work is nicely stated. But there is nothing in this text that is supposed to be taken in an opposite sense of the way it would naturally be understood. Hume is clearly concerned both about the potential general reaction to his essay and about avoiding accidental circulation of his argument before it is ready. His evaluation of its worth is not ironic (since the proposition that it would not be improper for the nameless use is certainly true), but rather diffident. What is on display in this passage is Hume's wit and modesty, two features which frequently appear in his writings. It is not, however, irony, in the specific sense of that which mean something different than what the natural sense implies.

On other occasions, Price mistakes sarcasm for irony. The distinction between these literary techniques is difficult since in some instances they overlap. When irony is used in a critical or judgmental manner, it can be sarcastic. If a football player drops an easy pass, and a fan shouts out, 'Great hands, buddy!!', this is clearly sarcastic irony. The opposite sense is intended, and that in a chastising way. However, not all sarcasm is ironic. Price quotes Hume's description of Cromwell's failings as a political leader and identifies it as ironic.[17]

This artful and audacious conspirator had conducted himself in the parliament with such profound dissimulation, with such refined hypocrisy, that he had long deceived those, who, being themselves very dexterous practitioners in the same arts, naturally entertained the more suspicion against others. (H 5.59.498)

Hume describes Cromwell (and the members of Parliament) as hypocritical, suspicious of others, dexterous politicians and (in Cromwell's case) a conspirator. These judgments are the natural sense of the text, and they are Hume's judgments. There is no reversal here, only dripping sarcasm.

Had Hume been writing in an ironic way, he might have composed this sentence in such a way that he applies terms like sincere or trusting to Cromwell, while cleverly intending the reader to understand just the opposite.

Hume, in fact, does deliver just such an ironic effect on many occasions, like this incident, also recorded in the *History*, in which Pope Clement VI made the 'fortunate islands' the domain of the Spanish monarch. The pope clearly meant the Canary Islands, then newly discovered, since 'canary' means fortunate. The British ambassador, however, because of deficient Latin skills, was 'seized with an alarm' since the British also considered their island fortunate. Hume offers this humorous judgment:

> Yet such was the ardour for study at this time, that Speed in his Chronicle informs us, that there were then 30,000 students in the university of Oxford alone. What was the occupation of all these young men? To learn very bad Latin, and still worse Logic? (H 2.16.283)

Several words and phrases in this passage are to be understood in the opposite sense. Clearly, 'the ardour for study' is intended irony for their lack of such, and the occupation of the Oxonians was certainly the reverse of learning 'very bad Latin and still worse Logic'. Hume's comments here are also sarcastic, as he issues a rather caustic commentary on the intellectual prowess of the students of the mid-14th century, but the distinction between what is sarcastic and what is ironic is straightforward.

The distinctions between circumstantial and rhetorical irony, and also between irony, sarcasm and wit are only the tip of iceberg in the complex literary seas of irony. To go further, it is necessary to enlist the aid of some experts in the field.

Irony in Literary Studies

The lack of critical deliberation on the nature of irony found in Hume scholarship is not mirrored in literary criticism. In fact, there is extensive reflection on the different kinds of irony and the nature of ironic expression in literary studies, and it can be profitably mined for interpreting Hume's own use of irony. In this section, I will report on some of the important distinctions and definitions from the literary study of irony and begin to explore some ways that these distinctions can help us to interpret Hume better.

Most literary discussions of the nature of irony begin with Roman scholars Quintilian and Cicero. The notion of irony was certainly known to the Greeks, but it is Cicero who first distinguished between an ironic remark and an ironic manner of being, and then identified Socrates as an example of the latter. 'Among the Greeks, history tells us, Socrates was fascinating and witty, a genial conversationalist; he was what the Greeks call εἴρων [eiron] in every conversation, pretending to need information and professing admiration for the wisdom of his companion.'[18] Quintilian advanced the understanding of irony with his definition that irony is a figure of speech in which one is 'asked to understand the opposite of what is said.'[19]

Throughout the medieval era and into the modern one, these and other aspects of Quintilian's analysis of irony served as important touchstones for a proper understanding of the phenomena of irony. Norman Knox, in his remarkably thorough study *The Word Irony and its Context, 1500–1755*, argues that in the time between Quintilian and the modern era little that was new was added to our understanding of the notion of the ironic, and that as a rhetorical device, it was predominantly used as a blame-through-praise or praise-through-blame strategy.[20] However, Knox holds that Quintilian's understanding of irony can be, at best, only introductory for a couple of reasons. One is that the moderns (beginning around the start of the 18th century) began to use the word in various circumstances and senses. The lexicography of these usages has proved to be tremendously complicated, but, nevertheless, a great benefit for interpreters of irony. Another problem with Quintilian's definition is that it does not sufficiently distinguish an ironic statement from a lie.

Here are some of the more important classifications Knox provides of the usages of *irony* during the 16th through 18th centuries.[21] The first is *Irony as Pretense and Deception*, which is intended deception and dissimulation. This one is a bit of a misnomer since it is more like lying or hypocrisy than irony. A second use is *Irony as Limited Deception*. The deception is only temporary, designed to produce the ironic effect on the readers, by clever use of language. One application of this kind of irony is the use of ambiguous language to conceal an aspect of the author's meaning from some members of the audience. Shaftesbury is mentioned as an individual who uses this kind of irony. Third, there is *Blame-by-Praise and Praise-by-Blame*. This use of irony is the most predominant, and is common in satire. Knox computes that about two-thirds of all uses of the word irony during the era he is studying refer to this playful kind of teasing or ridicule.[22]

Although more could be said about the various usages of the word *irony*, one question which emerges from this discussion is the use of irony as *deception* and the additional problems it raises for the interpreter. Many interpreters of Hume believe that Hume uses irony as a shield to hide his less than orthodox conclusions regarding God and religion. In order to evaluate this claim, more needs to be investigated regarding what irony is, what its purpose is and, then, ultimately, how to detect and interpret it.

Two contemporary attempts to define or delineate irony bear some review. The first of these is found in D. C. Muecke's book *The Compass of Irony*, where he argues that essential to any definition of irony are three elements. The first element Muecke describes as a double layer, that is, an upper and lower level to the irony.[23] In rhetorical irony, there is the surface meaning as it is initially apprehended by the hearer, and the true meaning that the ironist intends. In circumstantial irony, the same duality is present in the facts of the irony (which is the lower level) and the ironic take on the circumstances as recognized by an observer, which is the upper level.

For example, when one movie-goer said to her companion 'Great movie, right?' and then rolls her eyes, the intent is clear, even though the companion might have initially thought she really liked the movie prior to seeing the look of disgust. The lower level is the surface meaning, while the upper level is the truly intended meaning. A person caught cheating on her taxes is a straightforward state of affairs that becomes ironic when it is revealed that the tax cheat is an ethics professor who regularly lectures on the impermissibility of lying! The two points of view are often (although not necessarily) represented by two (or more) individuals who see the different perspectives. The ironist represents the upper level, while the hearer/reader is the lower level. Similarly, in the circumstantial irony of the tax-cheating ethics professor, she is the victim of the ironic state of affairs (the lower level), and those who smile knowingly at the irony inhabit the upper level.

Muecke's second element is that there must be some kind of opposition or antagonism between the two levels. If they are compatible, then there is no possibility for irony. He suggests that this opposition 'may take the form of contradiction, incongruity or incompatibility'.[24] This disconnect is what makes irony into the thing that it is. It is only when the individual at the lower level, by whatever means, suddenly realizes that some kind of incongruity is present and reverses course that she attains the second level and the ironic intent is recognized. This kind of communication is different from lying because the liar hopes that the hearer will never uncover the discrepancy, while in irony (especially rhetorical irony), the point is for the incongruity to be discovered and transcended, so the ironist and the hearer both inhabit the upper level.

The third element that Muecke observes is that there must be some kind of 'innocence' present, either a victim unaware of the ironic circumstances or ready to be taken in by the irony, even if briefly.[25] Identifying this innocence is another way of emphasizing the need for the disconnect. It is well illustrated by one of the more charming examples of irony that Muecke has gathered. In *Candide*, Voltaire writes of a particular battle that Candide observed, together with the circumstance that 'when all was over . . . the rival kings were celebrating their victory with Te Deums in their respective camps.'[26] The impossibility of both kings rightly claiming victory is made ironic by Voltaire's report of it. The reader chuckles in recognition of it, especially in picturing the earnest Te Deums in the camps, each blissfully unaware of the celebrations of the other side.

These three elements characterize what Muecke terms *simple irony*, and he offers the following definition. Simple irony is found when 'an apparently or ostensibly true statement, serious question, valid assumption, or legitimate expectation is corrected, invalidated or frustrated by the ironist's real meaning, by the true state of affairs or by what actually happened.'[27] Although lacking a genus, this definition does reflect the two-tiered aspect that Muecke highlights, with its attendant aspects of opposition between the two tiers and an innocent party. This definition also draws attention to another important aspect of irony, namely, that irony (at least, most kinds of irony) is intended to be understood and not remain mysterious or unresolved. This point is addressed in another part of Muecke's analysis, in which he divides simple irony into three grades or degrees: *overt irony, covert irony* and *private irony*.[28]

The spectrum ranges from overt irony, in which the hearer of irony understands almost immediately the true intent of the irony, to private irony, in which the ironist so well hides his true intent that it is inscrutable. The private ironist employs irony only for his own enjoyment, to the extent that, as Muecke observes, it comes close to being nothing more than a hoax.[29] By definition, private irony is hidden from all but the ironist, who is the only one who moves from the lower to the upper level.

Between overt and private irony is covert irony, and the line between covert and overt irony is, at once, clear and fuzzy. It seems relatively clear that covert irony is different from overt irony in that it is more difficult to detect. However, what is not so clear is just where the distinction is to be drawn, in order to make the difference meaningful. It is worthwhile to quote Muecke directly on this question:

What distinguishes Covert Irony [from Overt Irony] is that it is intended not to be seen but rather to be detected. The Covert Ironist will aim at avoiding any tone or manner or any stylistic indication that would immediately reveal his irony. The closer he can get to an 'innocent' non-ironical

way of speaking or writing while at the same time allowing his real meaning
to be detected the more subtle his irony. He must, of course, run the risk
of having his irony go undetected.[30]

Muecke, thus, sees the key distinction between covert and overt irony to be
the immediacy with which overt irony is recognized versus the process of
detection that must be undergone for covert irony to be discerned. How
this detection takes place is one of the most important aspects of the study
of irony. It is one thing to list and distinguish various types of irony or to
discuss and critique competing definitions and explanations of the ironic.
However, in order to make genuine progress in the project of interpreting
irony, it is necessary to explore means by which irony is intended to be
detected. The process of identifying and interpreting irony will be the topic
of the next section.

An example of covert irony includes the following sort of literary strategy.
A writer may take up the topic of abortion and offer a tepid defense of
the pro-life position. The irony is detected by those readers who know that
the writer is actually a published advocate of a pro-choice position, so what
looks like a weak defense of the antiabortion position is actually a tongue-
in-cheek advocacy of the pro-choice position by damning the opposition
with faint praise. It is covert irony, because it could be read as a straightforward defense of a particular point of view, but the careful reader, who
understands the fuller context of the author in question, detects the irony
and understands the true intent of the essayist.

It is appropriate to reflect on how the foregoing discussion applies to
Hume, particularly with regard to the three grades of irony that Muecke has
categorized. It seems to me that sometimes Hume's use of irony is overt
(consider the Canary Islands story above), but he is more likely to employ
some degree of covert irony. It seems highly implausible to me that Hume,
driven both to discover truth and then to share that truth with his readers,
would consistently wrap his views up in private riddles and enigmas that no
one could decipher. It seems overwhelmingly pointless for someone who
was as intent on challenging the intellectual status quo as Hume to engage
in such a private exercise. Private irony would also not be in keeping with
his mitigated skepticism.

It is my thesis that Hume used irony as a suitable vehicle for his wit, and
it also allowed him to take an edge off some of his controversial opinions,
while still communicating his various judgments to those readers who read
with care. This strategy is exactly what covert irony is. It is true, however,
that there are some who read Hume not as a covert ironist, but rather as

one who lies regarding his true beliefs in order to escape the wrath of his powerful opponents. This perspective seems inconsistent and self-defeating, but it will be evaluated more fully in a later section after the process for detecting and interpreting irony has been examined.

Detecting and Interpreting Irony

It is again helpful to begin with Quintilian in the important task of first detecting, and then interpreting irony. He identifies three factors to which a hearer must be alert in order to recognize that irony is in play. 'This [irony] is revealed either by delivery, by the character of the speaker or by the nature of the subject. If any of these is incompatible with the words, it is clear that the speech intends something totally different.'[31] In other words, Quintilian argues that the irony becomes obvious through the tone of the voice (a remark on the beautiful weather in a disgusted tone of voice indicates that the weather is not beautiful), or the inconsistency between the character of the speaker and the speech or the subject itself and the speech. For instance, if a known liberal congratulates George W. Bush on a political issue like capital punishment, it can be a clue that irony is likely in play. The third factor is when a speech is incongruous with the topic itself. The moderate, measured tone of Swift's 'A Modest Proposal' in the form of a serious essay is so inconsistent with the outrageous proposal that Irish babies should be eaten, that the irony is almost impossible to miss. Quintilian's analysis is that if any one of the factors is incongruous with the rest, then the hearer knows that the speaker's intent is ironic.

Muecke questions this final conclusion, arguing that at least two of these three factors need to be disconnected in order to be sure that irony is intended, since it is possible that the speaker may be somewhat inept, or perhaps a mistake has been made or maybe not enough is known about the speaker in order to know that irony is intended. For example, suppose that a college student writes an editorial in praise of Osama bin Laden, suggesting that he is a model citizen and just the kind of leader that we need for the 21st century. These statements are so incongruous that one may suspect irony or satire of the *Saturday Night Live* variety. However, it is possible that the student has mistaken bin Laden for someone else, or he misspoke in some manner, or even that he is a Muslim radical who truly believes that bin Laden has the correct answers to the problems of contemporary society.

It is on these grounds that Muecke's caution with regard to detecting irony is needed. It is often simply not that easy to be sure that someone has intended irony, especially in written communication or if little is known about the ironist. Spoken communication has certain advantages (tone, gestures, imitation) to help convey irony, which authors of written communication do not have. Comedy sketches like those on *Saturday Night Live* take full advantage of these characteristics of spoken communication. Certainly, however, authors are not without resources in this regard (once again, 'A Modest Proposal' is a stellar example), but it seems prudent to not be too hasty to identify irony in an author's writings unless a straightforward reading can be ruled out.

More guidance in this enterprise of identifying irony is provided by Wayne Booth in his book *A Rhetoric of Irony*. Booth's concern is a reconstruction of what he calls *stable irony*, which encompasses those instances in which the intended meaning of a passage is different from the natural sense of the passage, but, nevertheless, fixed and limited.[32] Booth holds that examples of stable irony are utterances that are covert (or hidden) in some sense, but with a stable (or fixed) meaning intended, so that there are not an infinite number of interpretations permissible. Muecke's covert irony and overt irony are both varieties of stable irony, since a specific interpretation is intended and the author provides the necessary clues to arrive at the proper interpretation. Private irony, however, is not stable, since the necessary interpretative helps are not provided. There are unstable ironies in which the ironist refuses to make any claims or to advance any propositions,[33] but, as was concluded above regarding private irony, unstable irony seems out of step with Hume's aims as a philosopher.

Were it the case that Hume was a complete Pyrrhonian skeptic, then the use of unstable irony would seem natural. Philosophy would become nothing but word games and elusive meanings. The only truth would be that no truths are knowable, so every philosophical treatise or essay is nothing but mocking irony. But this picture is not Hume. As a mitigated skeptic, he is cautious, believing that much of what has passed for knowledge in the past may not measure up against the standards that he imposes. Nevertheless, real knowledge is possible, and so there are real truths to be communicated. Irony has a place in this communication of truth, but not unstable irony. The preference is for those ironies whose reconstruction leads to a specific meaning.

Booth articulates four steps that must be followed in order to reconstruct rhetorical irony.[34] (1) Reject the natural sense of the proposition or expression as the likely meaning. (2) Weigh alternative meanings or circumstances (maybe a mistake was made or the author is unfamiliar with something that should be known). (3) Based on one's acquaintance with the author's beliefs or knowledge, render a judgment on whether irony is intended. (4) Reconstruct the intended meaning.

One of Booth's examples is the *Candide* excerpt noted above. When the reader reads that both armies celebrated a victory, it immediately raises doubts and questions. Can there be two victors in a battle? It seems not, so the reader is alerted to the possibility that there may be something more than just the simple surface meaning. The reader might wonder if Voltaire could have overlooked this fact. Was he careless or somehow naive about the nature of warfare? These conclusions seem unlikely, given Voltaire's intelligence. Further acquaintance with *Candide* reveals, however, that the book is replete with outrageous circumstances and foolish opinions. The whole book is a satirical journey through the 18th century, as Voltaire ridicules all that he finds shortsighted and backward in his world. In the context of the passage, Voltaire paints an ironic picture of supposed glories and honor of the military establishment of his day. Clearly, the correct reconstruction that the reader is intended to understand is Voltaire's contempt of the pomp and ceremony that surrounds the killing and suffering innate in warfare.

Reducing the process of identifying and reconstructing irony to these steps runs the risk of oversimplifying the process, a point with which Booth is acquainted. Steps 1 and 2 seem somewhat labored and obvious, since the reader (usually) accomplishes them in an instant. However, it is important to spell them out, if for no other reason than it focuses attention on Step 3, which is the most difficult part of interpreting irony. Unless one knows that the statement is intended as irony, there can be no hope of a correct reconstruction of the intended meaning. Once the reader realizes that irony is at play, the discovery of the intended alternate meaning generally (but not necessarily) follows with only a little thought. The most difficult interpretive task is being convinced that an ironic turn is being made. Therefore, it is necessary to explore a bit more of what happens at Step 3.

Booth describes five specific kinds of clues that an author can provide in order to help the reader to correctly identify the ironic utterances,[35] or, to use Muecke's language, to follow the ironist from the lower level to the upper level. First, the author may give clues in titles, epigraphs, disclaimers or other similar kinds of place. For example, when a leading scholar like Erasmus entitles a book *In Praise of Folly*, one is led to suspect some irony or satire. These kind of clues are straightforward, and helpful when supplied. Two other indicators of irony occur when a known error is proclaimed or the author contradicts himself in a particular work. A second indicator occurs when conventional wisdom is flaunted or historical facts misreported or an absurd premise asserted, one may suspect irony. As discussed above, the mere presence of these 'errors' is not sufficient to detect irony, but they are strong indicators.

A still stronger indicator occurs when the conflict occurs within the work in question or within the author's corpus. This third clue is especially relevant in interpreting Hume, since he publishes in his own name, but also in dialogues in which he hides behind the interlocutors. One valuable way to read the *Dialogues* and Section 11 of the first *Enquiry* is to look for assertions that either coincide or conflict with Hume's own positions. A conflict suggests that Hume may be speaking ironically through one of the characters in the dialogue.

The fourth clue that Booth suggests is an inconsistency in style and vocabulary. A sudden change in style is one way that an author of a written work can try to mirror or mimic the tonal clues that an ironic speaker has at her disposal. Obviously, the reader must have a great familiarity with the ironist in order for this kind of irony to be successful. Hume especially employs this kind of irony in his letters where he mocks piety or feigns anger.[36] It is harder to succeed at this kind of irony in a philosophical treatise, since the author does not know the reader or how alert an interpreter he or she may be. This problem highlights the fact that the author who uses stable or covert irony is responsible to provide sufficient clues so that the reader can interpret correctly. The unskilled ironist becomes, in effect, a private ironist (even if that is not the intent) if insufficient interpretive cues are not presented.

The last of Booth's clues is a conflict between what the author says and what the reader thinks are the author's true beliefs. In this circumstance, the reader is so familiar with the author's way of thinking that the reader is able to discern the true beliefs of the author (perhaps by 'reading between the lines') even if the true belief is never directly stated. This clue is, in my opinion, the one most prone to abuse. One of my purposes is to pay close attention to what Hume actually says, rather than to interpret his works according to the beliefs that we expect him to have. He never claims to be an atheist, yet many interpreters view the many passages where he affirms the existence of God to be ironic, simply because Hume could *not* have believed that. This kind of interpretation is not responsible, especially given the great pains Hume took to craft his books and essays. The same sort of care and attention to what the text says should guide his readers into recognizing both when he does and does not intend irony.

In summary, then, the interpreter of stable irony must recover the original intent of the ironist by recognizing the presence of irony and then reconstructing the proper meaning using the clues that the ironist supplies. Towards this end, Booth has supplied the interpreter of irony with these five clues to bear in mind.

Clue 1. The author provides explicit hints (titles, epigraphs, etc.) to indicate the use of irony.

Clue 2. The author asserts known errors.

Clue 3. The author contradicts himself or herself within his/her writings.

Clue 4. The style or vocabulary is inconsistent or incongruous relative to the meaning or the author's usual practice.

Clue 5. There is a conflict between the text as it is given and the author's known or expected beliefs.

Booth's list of clues is superior to Quintilian's earlier criteria in two regards. First, his list is longer and better suited specifically to written irony. Second, he avoids the mistake of suggesting that one clue is inevitably sufficient for the detection of irony. In cases where the irony is particularly subtle and covert, it is perhaps necessary for more than one clue to be present in order to confidently interpret the author's intent. At the very least, the more telling clues are needed. From Booth's list, the second and third clues are the most relevant for interpreting Hume, since they are based on locating the explicit conflict which signals irony. The last two clues, being less explicit, have reduced value, since it is questionable whether they alone are sufficient for the detection of irony. This judgment will have to await the inspection of specific texts.

Hume is not the only philosopher to use irony. Two masters of philosophical irony are Socrates and Soren Kierkegaard. The famous Socratic irony is displayed when he maintains his ignorance, keeping his Athenian conversation partners off balance while delighting and instructing centuries of philosophy students with his witty replies and clever critiques. Kierkegaard uses the guises of pseudonyms and other rhetorical devises to keep one step ahead of his readers and to demonstrate his ascendancy over others. In *The Concept of Irony*, Kierkegaard observes that one of the characteristics of irony is

a certain superiority deriving from its not wanting to be understood immediately, even though it [ultimately] wants to be understood, with the result that this figure looks down, as it were, on plain and simple talk that everyone can promptly understand; it travels around, so to speak, in an exclusive incognito and looks down pitying from this high position on ordinary, prosaic talk.[37]

Socrates uses irony because it is an excellent teaching tool and necessary for the effectiveness of his method. The reason why Kierkegaard uses irony is that it helps him achieve his literary agenda and to raise the level of intellectual discourse. To help understand Hume's use of irony, I turn to another master ironist – one who shared Hume's language, era and kingdom – Jonathan Swift.

The Irony of Jonathan Swift

A generation older than Hume, Swift was a writer that he admired and enjoyed.[38] So, despite the fact that Swift is not a philosopher, a quick investigation into his use of satire and irony will provide some useful context for understanding Hume. Swift, of course, is best known for his satirical novel *Gulliver's Travels*, which lampooned some of the cultural myopia of the day. Since, however, Hume did not write fiction, a more useful piece for comparison is Swift's famous essay 'A Modest Proposal' which makes the recommendation that the poverty-stricken Irish of his day sell their infant babies for food. So shocking and outrageous is this 'modest' proffer that it cannot possibly be taken seriously, despite the measured and rational tone of the essay as a whole. As such, it is a masterful example of extended irony, and one that will repay closer examination with some clues for detecting the use of irony.

The full title of Swift's essay is 'A Modest Proposal for Preventing the Children of poor People in Ireland, from being a Burden to their Parents or Country; and for making them beneficial to the Publick,'[39] and his stated thesis is that he is looking for a way to solve the problem of a couple of hundred thousand poor, starving Irish children who inevitably turn to begging and theft. Swift's persona (or *projector*) believes that he has happened upon a solution that will so well serve the Publick 'as to have his Statue set up for a Preserver of the Nation'.[40] His solution is that 100,000 Irish babies should be nursed for a year, at which point they will be (as an American friend has assured him) 'a most delicious, nourishing and wholesome Food'.[41] This course of action, Swift maintains, will yield a number of benefits. Primarily, the state of economic disadvantage (a surplus of children) is turned into a market advantage (a saleable commodity). Among the other benefits are a reduction in abortions and infanticides, an increase in marriages and an opportunity for economic gain among the poor, unskilled members of the society. There is also this service to the kingdom of England, namely, that this proposal, if enacted, would 'greatly lessen the *Number of Papists*, with whom we are yearly overrun'.[42]

Although written for the most part in the somber and systematic tone of a serious social commentary, this essay is clearly intended to be ironic because the thesis is so outrageous and shocking that it cannot be taken seriously on its face. In fact, the very reason that the humor of the piece is so successful is because of the jarring juxtaposition of the unconscionable proposal married to the staid, analytical way in which the proposal is advanced. This incongruity can be observed in another way. The projector's defense of his proposal is entirely economic, so much so, that the naive reader who happens to take him seriously, is enraged that Swift so blithely ignores the ethical hurdles regarding selling and eating human flesh. If Swift had tried to justify his cannibalistic proposal on moral grounds, his readers might be inclined to understand Swift to be sincere in his proposal. However, his blatant disdain for the most obvious counterargument highlights the outrageous nature of this plan, and it is the very outrageousness of the proposal that makes it ironic. It cannot be interpreted naturally as it stands.

There are, however, some other indications that Swift intends his essay to be understood ironically. First of all, there are some subtle hints dropped along the way which indicate that the essay falls far short of the rigor and precision that one expects of serious-minded calls for reform. One of these hints can be observed in Swift's discussion of the surplus of his commodity. He notes that infants will be more plentiful in March due to the greater amounts of fish (that 'prolifick Dyet') eaten by the Irish Catholics during Lent. The dubious fact that increased consumption of fish will lead to more offspring is furnished by an individual that Swift describes only as that 'grave Author',[43] but he is, in fact, the scandalous and ribald Rabelais, as Swift's more literate readers would recognize.

A second indication that Swift intends this essay to be understood ironically is that this essay stands at odds with other published opinions of Swift. Towards the end of the essay, the projector declaims that he can think of no objection that can be raised against this proposal unless it be argued that it will lessen the number of people in the kingdom of England. But, he argues, this objection is no objection at all, since the lessening of the population is the very thing that will solve the various problems of poverty and social unrest that existed at that time in Ireland. Swift says there are no meaningful objections to this modest proposal.

[L]et no man talk to me of other Expedients: *Of taxing our Absentees at five Shillings a Pound: Of using neither Cloaths, nor Household Furniture except what is of our own Growth and Manufacture: Of utterly rejecting the Materials and Instruments that promote foreign Luxury. . . .*[44]

The projector goes on at some length with this list of proposed reforms to which, he says, he will not hear, owing to the superior nature of his own modest proposal. What is not said, however, is that this roster of reforms are just the things that Swift has, in fact, in his own voice sincerely proposed as real solutions to the poverty-stricken conditions in Ireland.[45] If the present essay is not seen as ironic, this inconsistency between Swift's published comments regarding Irish poverty might be puzzling. In fact, however, this surface inconsistency actually increases interpretative clarity. The contrast between 'A Modest Proposal' and, for example, his 'Proposal for the Universal Use of Irish Manufactures' confirms the irony of the former, and the sincerity of the latter. Swift is using irony to sport with those who opposed his suggestions, by linking them with the outrageousness and preposterousness of his cannibalistic plan. Swift's ultimate goal is a serious one. It is only his means that are ironic and darkly humorous.

Swift's essay is a paradigm example of rhetorical irony because it exemplifies a number of Booth's clues for identifying irony. The outrageous claim offered in such serious language is clearly the incongruous language of Booth's 4th clue. Calling the ribald Rabelais a grave author and citing him as an authority on the reproductive advantages of fish are obvious examples of known errors being asserted, which is Booth's second clue. Finally, there are in 'A Modest Proposal' assertions which are directly contradictory to published claims of the author in other places. This last circumstance is precisely Booth's third clue, wherein the author contradicts himself or herself. The presence of these clues (especially more than one) allow us to confidently identify the piece on the whole as ironic, and then to reconstruct it in order to discern the author's intended meaning. Armed now with Booth's five clues and 'A Modest Proposal' as an example, it is time to return to Hume in order to see what can be said about detecting Hume's irony and discerning what his purposes are in employing this literary technique.

Discovering Hume's Irony

When Hume scholars do consider Hume's use of irony, the prevailing opinion is that he employs this literary device in order to hide his real beliefs. In other words, irony is meant as a cover or a facade, which may appease the more naive readers, while the more astute reader knows what Hume *really* means. Thus, Hume's irony both hides and reveals his intentions at the same time in a way that is different from the covert irony discussed above. Covert irony employs a momentary diversion, but anticipates all attentive readers making the interpretive move to the ironic level of meaning. By contrast, this *covering* irony is intended to communicate different things to different readers.

One individual who understands Hume's use of irony in this way is M. A. Box in his book *The Suasive Art of David Hume*,[46] which investigates the literary characteristics and developments in Hume's corpus. Box acknowledges that Hume has a constructive, positive philosophical project which uses mitigated skepticism as the means to that goal. However, according to Box, this positive project stops short when it comes to religious inquiry.

> What he was willing to call 'true religion' was with regard to divinity so attenuated by agnostic reservations as to be unrecognizable as religion by most people. While no one, perhaps, has yet been able to codify definitively what exactly it was that Hume called true religion, few readers have not been able to see through his ironic genuflexions. This mixture of obscurity and transparency is undoubtedly just about what Hume intended.[47]

The premise that Hume intended to be obscure regarding the exact nature of true religion is significant for Box, since he ultimately concludes not only that Hume is a religious agnostic, but also that this agnosticism is precisely the position that Hume's works on religion advocates.

In a section entitled 'Ironic Coyness', Box presents the following argument for a 'dual persona' approach to understanding Hume's irony. The first persona is an 'inept apologist' who does more harm than help to the Christian cause. He 'is ludicrously unaware of the wounds that he inflicts on his own cause, while the reader knows perfectly well that Hume is manipulating him into embarrassments.'[48] It is through the inept failures of this persona that Hume advances, using irony as a sword, in an offensive posture against the dogmas of the false religion. However, owing to the times, in which religious persecution was still an option, Box sees Hume building walls of defense by use of the second persona, which is the fideist.[49] At the moments when the first persona is ironically making such a mess of the religious point of view that the faithful are ready to begin official sanctions, the fideist persona emerges to make pious declamations of the mysteries of faith and the need to remain loyal to the received Christian tradition. As Box observes, 'No one might believe these professions of faith, but no one could prove them insincere either.'[50] The purported beauty of this strategy is that Hume is able to cleverly and ironically appear to be defending the faith, when in point of fact, he is revealing its philosophical weaknesses and irrationality. Box concludes, 'For the interpreter of the whole *oeuvre* [of Hume], Hume the fideist and Hume the deist cancel each other out, leaving only Hume the doubting Thomas.'[51]

The support for this interpretive scheme lies in seeing the grand scale of Hume's irony, the whole of Hume's corpus, since these personae are not explicitly contrasted. According to Box, the first *Enquiry* reflects the fideistic persona, while the *Natural History* captures Hume in his deistic guise. On more controversial religious issues (like miracles and the immortality of the soul), Hume's agnostic empirically based conclusions run the greatest risk of public outcry, and so here the duel of the personae is most apparent. The pious declamations of the fideist are placed in close context with counter-thrusts of the skeptic, leaving only agnosticism. This dialectic is best seen in Hume's essays about miracles and the immortality of the soul. In both essays, there is an appeal to faith found in close context with philosophical conundrums.

In response to Box's thesis, however, a few objections may be raised. First, it is not precisely clear what a persona that is both deist and apologist is supposed to represent, since the two terms are not synonymous. Next, Box does not support his claim that the first *Enquiry* is fideistic, while the *Natural History* is deistic. On the surface, this characterization seems intriguing, but absent the textual support for such a sweeping generalization, the thesis is not very compelling, especially since the irony of these different personae must extend over different published works. Finally, the whole dialectic of the two personae, with all of its feints and diversions, is rather complex and mysterious, especially given that the entire enterprise lives between the lines and beneath the surface. It is certainly not obvious to me that Box's complicated interpretive scheme is the most plausible construal of Hume's intentions. Let me propose a simpler reading of one of these texts.

On the essay 'Of the Immortality of the Soul', Box correctly observes that the first and last paragraphs have a kind of fideistic quality, whereas the rest of the essay in the middle is much more skeptical and philosophical regarding the possibility of the soul's immortality.

In these passages, Hume asserts that it is 'the gospel, and the gospel alone, that has brought life and immortality to light'. (E IS, 590) He concludes that 'nothing could set in a fuller light the infinite obligations, which mankind have to divine revelation; since we find, that no medium could ascertain this great and important truth.' (E IS, 598) The point of the essay is that Hume has examined all the metaphysical, moral and physical arguments for the immortality of the soul and found them wanting. If, indeed, we as humans are to know or believe that our soul will survive death, it can only be on account of divine revelation. This conclusion is the natural reading of the text, and this conclusion squares with Hume's point of view. It is clear from Hume's deathbed conversation with Boswell that he did not so believe.

While at first blush, these texts may appear wholly ironic and disingenuous, a closer look will reveal that Hume's irony here is mild, and that much of what is asserted in these paragraphs is consistent with the positions that Hume takes in other places. Hume's strategy is to offer a position that both he and the believers can accept, namely, that the best argument for the immortality of the soul is the testimony of Scripture. That Hume stops short of explicitly stating his disbelief only means that he delicately ended his essay at a place where he made his point (that empirical philosophy does not support the belief in the soul's immortality) without explicitly antagonizing Christian believers.

Of course, the attentive reader who has read widely in Hume's corpus will know that there is much here that is unsaid. His description of the doctrine of a future state as 'this great and important truth' is surely disingenuous. When Hume asserts that the best argument for the doctrine is divine revelation, he is damning with faint praise. Another telltale sign of irony is Hume's mention of the 'infinite obligations' that mankind has in light of divine revelation. This statement is certainly at odds with his secularly based ethics, and it reveals Hume to be certainly ironic and playful in his analysis of the matter at hand.

Given these ironic elements and Hume's lack of complete disclosure, how is one to analyze this passage and the essay as a whole? It is understandable that some conclude that Hume is being cleverly deceptive to the degree that nothing that he writes is as it seems. This approach is characteristic of those who espouse the conventional story and hold that any positive religious assertion from Hume should be disregarded as deceptive and insincere. However, this reading of Hume is not necessitated by the texts. It is not inconsistent for Hume to admit that the strongest and best arguments for the immortality of the soul come from the Bible. That he does not hold the Bible as true or authoritative is clear, but the point of the essay is not to debate the veracity of these sources. In fact, the argument concerns the empirical evidences for the immortality of the soul, for which Hume finds none. The true significance of what Hume said and did not say can be seen better if the essay is viewed in its historical setting.

As will be shown in the next chapter, the intellectual context within which Hume worked was exceedingly complex. Hume was not simply challenging Christians who believed in the immortality of the soul, but operated within a rich and varied range of intellectual positions on matters theological, philosophical and social. On the particular issue of the immortality of the soul, Hume was in at least partial agreement (surprisingly enough) with more fideistic believers, who based their beliefs on the assertions of Scripture and not on the discoveries of reason. Both Hume and the fideists agreed that the arguments for the immortality of the soul being what they are, if one believes, one does so on the basis of divine revelation. Those who disagreed with this point of view were the more intellectually minded believers (like, for example, some of the English deists), who believed that the doctrine of the immortality of the soul can be established on the basis of natural theology. Hume was clearly at odds with these individuals, and the astute members of this group understood the clever way in which Hume divided the believing population in response to his essay. It is not beyond imagination to picture Hume, who loved to joke and tease, enjoying his brief allegiance with more conservative Christians, while he is, at the same time, spiting the philosophical arguments on their more intellectual brethren.

In spite of the teasing, however, it is clear that Hume is not being deceitful or employing some version of private irony in the things that he asserts. These texts provide us with a clear example of covert, stable irony, which require a bit of attention and understanding on the part of the reader in order to appreciate the full significance of what Hume is communicating. Thus, I fail to see in this essay any necessity for Box's complicated dual-personae model to correctly interpret this essay. What is necessary, however, is a thorough understanding of what irony is, and a hermeneutical approach that provides a method for correctly interpreting it.

Another strategy for understanding Hume's irony is to link him with the deists and free-thinkers of the early 18th century, who also had reason to challenge the religious status quo, but faced the possibility of persecution if they were deemed a heretic or blasphemer. Isabel Rivers argues that irony and equivocation were, therefore, two of the deists' chief means of expressing themselves, allowing them to walk the tricky path of religious dissent in this era:

> Irony and equivocation, for example, may be used not so much to *conceal* views as to reveal them in a certain way. The purpose may be to entrap the reader while leaving the writer an escape route. Writer and reader may be drawn into an alliance (willing or unwilling on the latter's part) in which they both know very well what the writer is up to. Further, these tactics may be part of a carefully worked out theory of exoteric and esoteric

doctrines which assumes two audiences who are either addressed separately in different works in a language appropriate to them, or expected
to respond to the same work in two different ways.[52]

Such an approach makes it very difficult for the reader to correctly ascertain just what the author thinks on the topic at hand, a point not lost on
those who were troubled by the free-thinking trend. Defenders of orthodox
Christianity, like George Berkeley and Samuel Clarke, denounced these
duplicitous tactics, because they muddied the difficult theological waters
and made it hard to say with assurance just what the deists believed.[53]
Of course, the deists held that it was necessary to engage in this kind of
'raillery' in order to escape persecution. Shaftesbury is often quoted in this
regard:

> If Men are forbid to speak their minds seriously on certain Subjects, they
> will do it ironically. If they are forbid to speak at all upon such Subjects,
> or if they find it really dangerous to do so; they will then redouble their
> Disguise, involve themselves in Mysteriousness, and talk so as hardly to be
> understood, or at least not plainly interpreted, by those who are dispos'd
> to do 'em a mischief. And thus *Raillery* is brought more in fashion, and
> runs into an Extreme.[54]

David Berman believes that this kind of raillery is better understood as
theological lying as opposed to irony, since this kind of speech is intended to
communicate two different things to two different audiences.[55] The one
which actually corresponds to the author's intent is the *esoteric* (or private)
message, while the one which cleverly miscommunicates his intent to the
other group is *exoteric* (or public) message. Berman argues that all the significant deists (Collins, Tindal, Toland, Blount, Shaftesbury among others),
including Hume and Locke, engage in theological lying in order to pursue
some of their controversial religious conclusions. Berman wonders, however, if they are indeed lying, then how can we know what they really
thought? It means that the reader must already know the authors have nonorthodox beliefs in order to receive the esoteric message. So why go to all
the trouble to esoterically communicate to people who already are part of
the private group?

In order to resolve this puzzle, Berman proposes that there is a third intent
beyond the exoteric and the esoteric. The third level is *insinuation*, which is
the implication to unwary readers that some particular religious doctrine
(like immortality) is more questionable and ridiculous than they originally

thought.[56] In other words, there is some kind of persuasion going on, in which the deists are trying to quietly win more adherents to their views.

Given the complexity of this analysis, one may wonder how often the deists were successful at communicating to their audiences, if indeed at all. Whether it is theological lying, equivocation or insinuation, the goal is to deceive and to cover one's intentions. How is it possible that one can communicate one's views on a particular topic when one is trying to conceal them? Even if occasionally one hits on a clever turn of phrase that has an element of double-entendre to it, the author who is committed to writing in this manner is condemning himself to an imprecise and ill-understood message. The stable ironist uses irony, but intends a specific meaning and provides clues to reach that meaning. The theological liar severely hinders his ability to write with precision and to make fine distinctions. He is never able to qualify a point or distinguish himself from a close ally, since these deviations become still more lies or equivocations. Thus, he restricts himself to broad positions and generalizations only, since it is not possible to examine a particular issue with precision and finesse, while still maintaining the two levels of meaning. The result is that the whole enterprise of exoteric and esoteric communication has a paradoxical element, as Rivers acknowledges. She says, 'If irony is to be protective, then it must be ambiguous; but if ridicule is to differentiate truth from imposture, then its object must be understood.'[57] It is not clear whether this fundamental inconsistency can be consistently overcome.

James Fieser, in an article that focuses primarily on Hume,[58] tries to avoid the problem of theological lying by asserting that Hume primarily attempts to *conceal* his controversial religious views, at least judging by the mixed interpretation of Hume by his contemporaries. William Warburton, for instance, opines that in the *Natural History* Hume is making progress towards believing in God. He writes, 'And here let me observe it to his honour that, tho' he be not yet got to THEISM, he is however of the advance and approaching to the borders of it.'[59] However, George Horne, another of Hume's reviewers, disputes Warburton's analysis of Hume's religious beliefs. 'In the *Natural History of Religion* . . . [Warburton] thought our philosopher was approaching towards the *borders of Theism.* But I never could find that he penetrated far into the *country.*'[60] Fieser notes that a spectrum of interpretations regarding what Hume thought exists today, even as it did in Hume's day, although he also believes that a little reflection can uncover Hume's concealed views. If that analysis is accurate, then the proper picture is to view Hume more like a covert ironist than a theological liar. The presence of a multiplicity of views regarding what Hume really thought means only that some have not understood him properly, not that he necessarily intended to deceive or cover his views.

At the end of a long review of the myriad of questions on irony and Hume's use of it, it is time to offer some final evaluations. What kind of an ironist is Hume and what is the best way to understand his use of irony? Some words on the topic from Hume himself are revealing. In the *Treatise*, there is a lengthy reflection on the advantage of satire as an indirect means of criticism. Although he speaks explicitly of satire, it seems to me that what he says applies also to the use of irony.

> Every one knows, there is an indirect manner of insinuating praise or blame, which is much less shocking than the open flattery or censure of any person. However he may communicate his sentiments by such secret insinuations, and make them known with equal certainty as by the open discovery of them, 'tis certain that their influence is not equally strong and powerful. One who lashes me with conceal'd strokes of satire, moves not my indignation to such a degree, as if he flatly told me I was a fool and coxcomb; tho' I equally understand his meaning, as if he did. This difference is to be attributed to the influence of general rules. (T 1.3.13.13)[61]

Two important insights are to be gained regarding Hume's understanding of irony. First, the ironist and the non-ironist are, in the end, both communicating the same message. The only difference is the means. Hume says that he *equally* understands the meaning. Thus, what Hume has in mind is stable irony. The second insight concerns what Hume sees as the purpose of irony, which is that it is a matter of politeness and social grace. If one can soften one's criticism in such a way that it avoids the bald use of names or open censure, this option is more pleasing and acceptable in society. There is no mention here of concealing beliefs or creating a diversion. Instead, the concern is proper conduct. While Hume does not explicitly say that this is the purpose behind his *own* use of irony, it certainly fits the reading that I proposed above regarding 'Of the Immortality of the Soul'. Despite his nonorthodox beliefs, Hume maintained good relations with numerous clergy and Christian friends.[62] The friendships were not sacrificed because of theological differences. Hume considered it a mark of a civilized person that they could disagree with dignity and respect.

This way of understanding Hume's purpose for the use of irony fits also with his disdain for enthusiasm and dogmatism, angry debates and fiery pamphlets. One of the important differences that separates Hume from the free-thinkers like Collins and Toland is that they were radicals, eager for a debate and anxious to provoke angry outcries. Hume abhorred this sort of emotional polemic (cf. T 1.3.13.15–18). What scholars like Berman and Fieser (and others who lump Hume together with the free-thinkers) overlook is that, while there may be some similarities in terms of their beliefs, there is a wide gulf between them in terms of their social standing. Hume was the famous historian and essayist, a diplomat and university librarian, and the friend of Smith and d'Holbach and Franklin. He moved in circles of influence, and the tactics of the free-thinkers were beneath him. Hume disliked angry denunciations of others and never responded to similar kinds of criticisms of his positions. His writings are cautious and measured, the product of careful reflection and multiple revisions, and the very antithesis of the pamphlets and angry reviews which characterize much of what went for discussion during his lifetime.[63] The opinion of Sir Leslie Stephen, in his oft-referenced *History of English Thought in the Eighteenth Century*, is instructive, if a bit pejorative, on this point:

> It would be difficult to mention a controversy in which there was a greater disparity of force. The physiognomy of the books themselves bears marks of the difference. The deist writings are but shabby and shrivelled little octavos, generally anonymous, such as lurk in the corners of dusty shelves, and seem to be the predestined prey of moths. Against them are arrayed solid octavos and handsome quartos and at times even folios – very Goliaths among books, too ponderous for the indolence of our degenerate days, but fitting representatives of the learned dignitaries who compiled them.[64]

Given all these differences between Hume and those engaged in raillery, it is hard to conceive of Hume using irony primarily as a means to lie or deceive. Irony for Hume is part of the craft of good writing, and a necessary tool in order to soften his critiques of the positions of others. It is not primarily a tool used to undermine the clear communication of his ideas and conclusions.

A Hermeneutic for Irony

Given all that has been said regarding the nature of irony, the various kinds of irony, the purposes of irony and how one may detect and reconstruct irony, it is time to synthesize all these elements together into a hermeneutic for Hume's irony, that is, a procedure for interpreting his use of irony. This process begins with the recognition that rhetorical irony is a figure of speech that employs a bi-level means of communication. The first level is the natural sense of the proposition, but the ironist, by building some form of incongruity into the text, clues the reader that some differing sense is intended. Although there are private or unstable ironies that are intended only for the ironist, in general, the ironist's desire is that the reader follow through to the intended meaning. These kinds of stable ironies can range from the readily overt and transparent varieties to the more covert and subtle. I have argued that Hume's use of irony is generally covert and stable, requiring some thought from his readers in order to both identify and decipher his ironic statements.

1. Given that Hume's use of irony is presumably stable and covert, the reader of Hume must be alert to the possibility of irony and prepared to search for clues that will suggest that intention.

The purposes of irony are many. For some, it is an opportunity to display superior intelligence or literary ability, as Kierkegaard suggested. Some may attempt to use it as a way to communicate to some select readers, while deceiving others, although, as I have argued, the possibility for success using this strategy seems low. Still others (like Voltaire) employ it as a way to display sarcasm or ridicule, or, after Socrates, as a dialectic for training young minds. Yet again, there are those for whom irony is a mark of good writing, a way to soften criticism and to take the edge off controversial conclusions. I have argued that, for Hume, irony is primarily used in accord with this last purpose, especially in his published works.

2. The reader of Hume must recognize that irony generally serves two purposes for Hume, namely, to soften the criticism of those with whom he disagrees, for propriety's sake, and also to serve as an avenue for Hume's wit and humor, even in his published works.

The key to detecting irony is to pay attention to the clues which the ironist supplies and which highlight the incongruity that is at the heart of irony. Some authors supply explicit hints that irony is intended, and others are so well-known as ironists that the readers need some explicit instructions when the author is not being ironic! Thus, paying attention to the clues that a stable ironist provides is perhaps the most important of the hermeneutical principles for discerning irony.

3. In order to properly detect and interpret irony, the reader of Hume should be alert for these five clues:

   Clue 1. The author provides explicit hints (titles, epigraphs, etc.) to indicate the use of irony.
   Clue 2. The author asserts known errors.

Clue 3. The author contradicts himself or herself within his/her writings.

Clue 4. The style or vocabulary is inconsistent or incongruous relative to the meaning or the author's usual practice.

Clue 5. There is a conflict between the text as it is given and the author's known or expected beliefs.

As I indicated above, the last two of these five clues require some caution in application. It is well-known that Hume is a careful writer and creative thinker, and a philosopher who does not necessarily draw the same conclusions as others. Thus, the safest interpretive path is to pay close attention to what Hume actually says and to resist the urge to take Hume past what he explicitly asserts. The passages from 'Of the Immortality of the Soul' serve as a suitable example of this caution. There is irony in what Hume says regarding, for instance, our human obligations growing out of divine revelation. However, not every religious proposition that he asserts is automatically to be viewed as disingenuous or insincere.

4. Once the irony is detected, the last step for the reader is to reconstruct the meaning of the passage in question in order to identify Hume's true intent. If the first three steps have been followed correctly, the last step is able to be completed in a straightforward manner.

Chapter 3

Hume and Deism

Introduction to the Problem

It has been commonplace among recent interpreters of David Hume to name him a deist.[1] As has already been discussed, this trend is largely the result of J. C. A. Gaskin's influential analysis of Hume's philosophy of religion, in which Gaskin concludes that Hume is an *attenuated deist*. Briefly stated, the story of this appellation runs as follows. Interpreters of Hume contrast the repeated deity-affirming passages in his corpus with the skeptical empiricism that is the foundation of his epistemology, and conclude that Hume, at most, retains a residual theism. Finding historical deism conveniently located in (roughly) the same place and time as Hume, the identification is naturally made that Hume's deity is some shallow version of the inactive god of the deists. The following quotation reflects this kind of analysis:

> Hume's final position in the philosophy of religion is both deflationary and ironic. It is deflationary in that the strongest position he is prepared to accept on the total evidence is a very weak form of deism. But even his acceptance of that is hedged with conditions. Briefly, deism is the view that there is an original supernatural source of the universe, but, while this source is perhaps a personal agent of some sort, with a mind somehow resembling ours, there is not sufficient reason to think such a being is all good, or even overall good, or cares about us. But Hume does not accept even as much as this generic form of deism. For he is convinced that the facts of this world give us good reason, not just to not endorse, but to *reject* the idea that the supernatural source of the universe, if any [such being exists], is good or cares about us.[2]

It is my view that this analysis misconstrues Hume's theism. First, it undercuts the importance of the affirmation texts in Hume. Second, it betrays a fundamental misunderstanding regarding the nature of deism, which, when corrected, shows popular deism to be anachronistically linked to Hume. Third, this position ignores several critical differences between Hume and the English deists. The positive character of just how Hume conceives the deity is reserved for Chapters 4 and 5, but this chapter will address the second and third objections.

Popular Deism and English Deism

The exact nature of deism has always been notoriously difficult to identify. In 1920, a careful scholar could begin an inquiry into the topic with this statement, 'There is no accepted definition of Deism,' and in 1960, another commentator could devote an entire article to the question whether the deists were, in fact, deists.[3] The same difficulties that were noted in the last century are still with us today, and part of the conceptual difficulty stems from the fact that there are two distinct ways in which the concept of deism is misunderstood. The first of these problems is a conflation of historical deism with what some commentators call *philosophical deism*, or, to use the phrase that I prefer, *popular deism*. This distinction can be easily drawn, but it continues to be ignored in many circles, including Hume studies. The second problem is the more vexing one, since it involves giving an account of the rather unruly and chaotic era of the deistic debates in England, Scotland and Ireland. In order to truly understand David Hume's relationship to this movement, it is necessary to address both of these issues.

There is no terminological consensus among those who acknowledge the distinction that I have been advocating between the rather simple deism of the absentee god and the historical English deism. The term *philosophical deism* is too broad and potentially misleading since the historical deists (English and otherwise) were also concerned with philosophical matters. William Rowe distinguishes between deism 'in the proper sense', referring to the historical movement, and deism 'in the popular sense', by which he means that variety of theism that imagines a god who creates, but nevertheless exercises no providential care over his creation.[4] Following Rowe's lead and (at least in part) his terminology, I will make the careful distinction between *popular deism*, by which I mean the belief in the notion of an absentee, nonprovidential deity, and *English deism*, which refers to the historical movement of thinkers from the British Isles who shared a common agenda, during the 17th and 18th centuries. Historically, there is also *French deism* and *American deism*, and although there are some commonalities within the three traditions, there are also significant differences. The English deists arrive earlier in history and also are not as anti-Christian as their French and American cousins.

The core idea behind popular deism is that the creator of all things maintains a causal distance from his creation. In other words, the deity does not actively involve himself in the day-to-day guidance and governance of the world by answering prayers or performing miracles or doing other acts of providence. This view emphasizes the transcendence of God and de-emphasizes his immanence in the world. It is, thus, at odds with the traditional Christian conception which understands God to be both beyond the creation, but also active in the world. A popular analogy for this 'absentee' deity is of a clock-maker who constructs and winds the clock in such a way that it operates in perpetuity without need of constant attention. This conception of deism is often attributed to the English deists of the 18th century. Here is an example, taken from church historian Henry Daniel-Rops:

> Deism, born in England and spread abroad partly by the anglomania of that age, retained a God, but a God remote, pale and shadowy, never intervening in human affairs and demanding no act of faith. His existence was arrived at by a simple process of reasoning: no watch without a watchmaker. But this unknown God, who was beginning to be called 'the Supreme Being', was not credited with any attribute apart from existence. If he imposed a religion at all, it was natural religion, as old as the world, embracing all the creeds without distinction and sufficiently vague to rouse the fervour of M de Voltaire.[5]

If there be any truth to this analysis, it is only if it is applied (with qualification) to a later place and time than the British Isles of the late 17th and early 18th centuries. The god that Daniel-Rops describes is not the god of the classic English deists, whose pamphlets fired the intellectual debates of Britain during the childhood of Hume. The more skeptical French *philosophes*, like Voltaire and Diderot, together with American deists like Thomas Paine and Elihu Palmer, did tend towards the position that Daniel-Rops describes, but these thinkers belong to the second half of the 18th century or later.

Clearly, one cannot deny that there were and are individuals who conceived of the deity in this absentee manner, nor could one hold the position that such a conception is without philosophical merit in the spectrum of ideas. However, the point that must be insisted upon is that this popular deism is *not* the deism that came to the center of the intellectual stage during the early part of Hume's life, that is, during the time of the English deists. To fail to make this distinction between the rather simplistic popular deism and the complex and contradictory positions of the English deists is to perpetuate a rather grievous anachronism, as Hefelbower and Winnett are both quick to point out.[6] Put another way, popular deism is a specific way of imagining the role of the deity in the universe, while English deism is a movement in which the individual deists developed an entire religious worldview around the various points of their agenda. Of course, it is possible for a historical deist to hold to the belief in an absentee deity as one aspect of his larger worldview, but that does not negate the distinction.

These historical points of order are important since Gaskin's conclusion that Hume was an attenuated deist is built on the idea that popular deism and English deism are one. Gaskin and O'Connor clearly understand deism to be a middle point between theism and atheism, and see Hume's position on the existence of God to be between deism and atheism. Thus, Gaskin argues that Hume is an attenuated deist.

> So my contention is that Hume gives some sort of genuine assent to the proposition *that there is a god.* This assent that 'lyes in the middle' is between deism and atheism. It is fostered by the feeling of design and given a weak rational basis by recognition that the order to be found in nature *could* (not must) be explained by the work of an ordering agent. But this ordering agent – and this is the aspect of the *Dialogues* which easily deceives those in search of Hume's theism or his atheism – cannot be known to have any attributes other than those just sufficient to produce the given result; that is to say, the power of an agent together with 'some remote analogy to human intelligence'.[7]

So, it is clear that for Gaskin, deism is popular deism, since he places it in the spectrum between atheism and theism. This identification would not be a problem if the English deists also understood the deity in this way, but this is not the case. Whether popular deism coincides with any historically significant figures prior to the 20th century is a question I will not investigate, but I have my doubts.

Although Hume was acquainted with many of the leading French deists, they understood that he did not share their theological conclusions regarding the nature of God. Several quotations bear witness to this fact, including the famous story of Hume's conversation about atheists with the French thinker Baron d'Holbach. There are many accounts of this story (which do not all agree with each other), but the one recounted by Denis Diderot seems the most historically accurate:

> The first time that M. Hume found himself at the table of the Baron, he was seated beside him. I don't know for what purpose the English

philosopher took it into his head to remark to the Baron that he did not believe in atheists, that he had never seen any. The Baron said to him: 'Count how many we are here.' We are eighteen. The Baron added: 'It isn't too bad a showing to be able to point out to you fifteen at once: the three others haven't made up their minds.'[8]

Gaskin himself acknowledges the gap between the French deists and Hume, and quotes a letter sent home by a British expatriate in France, that 'poor Hume, who on your side of the water was thought to have too little religion, is here thought to have too much.'[9] Voltaire also indicated his disagreement with Hume on the question of the deity. He observed that Hume's thesis that polytheism was the original religious inclination of primitive man (from the *Natural History*) was at odds with the English and French deistic conclusion that a single supreme god is known through nature and has always thus been known, even before the beginning of the Judeo-Christian tradition.[10]

Gaskin seems unaware of the fact that the English deists were not proponents of popular deism as such. He does mention some of the main English deists (Lord Herbert of Cherbury, John Toland, Matthew Tindal and Charles Blount) and indicates their concern with questions of natural religion versus revealed religion, their opposition to the priesthood, and their reflections on the theological issues of prophecy and miracles.[11] What he does not mention is that the English deists, for the most part, did not waver on the question of the existence of God. Nor does he address the rich list of divine attributes that most English deists discovered via natural religion. In mentioning these English deists, he implies that Hume's alleged attenuated deism is a variety of their deism, but this connection cannot be substantiated. The attenuated deism that Gaskin proposed has only a passing resemblance to the English deism of the late 17th and early 18th centuries.

Gaskin's problem is one that he shares with others who try to identify Hume with the English deists of the early 18th century, and it is that he offers a far too simplistic understanding of a rather complex set of issues and problems, both historical and conceptual. The absentee god of popular deism is a reductivistic simplification of the complex theological and philosophical issues that characterized the deistic controversy in England during this era. Both those who are termed deists and their various opponents deserve better treatment than this anachronistic attempt to over-simplify their beliefs with the terms and concepts of our much more secular and much less theologically sophisticated era. In order to dispel this misunderstanding, it is necessary to give a responsible account of the intellectual climate of this age, and the real issues and problem of the English deist debate.

The Context of English Deism

One of the leading British intellectuals at the beginning of the 18th century was Samuel Clarke. A disciple of Newton and an accomplished metaphysician, Clarke was heavily involved in all the theological discussions of the era. Invited to give the prestigious Boyle Lectures in both 1704 and 1705, [12] Clarke addressed the topic of natural theology. In these lectures, he famously catalogued four different kinds of deists, all of which, according to Clarke, believed in God and identified him as the eternal, infinite and all-wise creator of the universe. What distinguishes the different groups from each other is their agreement or dissent from a list of debated topics. The first group rejects any notion of providence in the universe, believing that 'God does *not at all concern* himself in the *Government* of the World, nor has any regard to, or care of, what is done therein.'[13] This group comes the closest to the popular deism of a later age, but the English deists of this first group confess to a greater list of divine attributes than what Gaskin allows.[14] Clarke observed that this group of deists were trying to base their opinions on the laws of motion which Newton recently discovered, but that they had, in fact, mistaken the implications of those laws.

> Those Men [the first group of deists] indeed, who, merely through a certain vanity of Philosophizing, have been tempted to embrace that other Opinion, of all things being produced and continued only by a *certain Quantity of Motion originally* impressed on *Matter* without any determinate Design or Direction, and left to it self to form a World at adventures; Those Men, I say, who, merely through the vanity of Philosophizing, have been tempted to embrace that Opinion, without attending whither it would lead them. . . . But 'tis certain, that Many under that cover, have really been Atheists; and the *Opinion it self* (as I before said) leads *necessarily*, and by unavoidable consequence, to *plain Atheism*.[15]

The second group does hold to the providence of God and his power and wisdom, but denies him any moral characteristics. As a result, there is no divine law, no consequences for good or evil actions, and the notions of good and evil are found to be nothing but human constructions. In addition, deists of this type are opposed to any Christian revelation or moral obligation.[16] The third set of deists acknowledges the existence of God and ascribes to him all the traditional divine qualities, including the moral perfections that were denied by the second group. This third group, however, rejects any future state. In Clarke's words, 'But then, having a prejudice against the Notion of the *Immortality of Human Souls*, they believe that Men perish intirely at Death, and that one Generation shall perpetually succeed another, without any thing remaining of Men after their departure from this Life, and without any future restoration or renovation of things.'[17] Clarke believes that, like the first group of deists, the second and third groups also ultimately reduce to atheism, and that, in fact, the number of people who hold to these teachings are few.

The final group that Clarke classifies accepts the same traditional list of divine attributes as the third group and also holds to the existence of an immortal soul, a life to come and eternal rewards and punishments. What differentiates them from orthodox Christians is that this fourth group discovers all these truths solely on the basis of natural religion and rejects the need for any divinely given written revelation.

> But All this [the divine attributes], the Men we are now speaking of, *profess to believe* only so far as 'tis discoverable by the Light of Nature alone; without believing any Divine Revelation. These, I say, are the only *True Deists*; and indeed the only Person who ought in reason to be argued with in order to convince them of the Reasonableness, Truth and Certainty of the *Christian Revelation*.[18]

The reason that Clarke holds that these are the only true deists is because there is nothing wrong with *what* they believe, only with the *method* and *grounds* by which they profess to come to that truth. Clarke believes that the other three groups of deists are really atheists in disguise, but that this last group would be Christians, if only they would acknowledge the necessity of the Bible.

Clarke's analysis is significant, but not necessarily because there really were these different groups of thinkers as such. He does not name individuals who would fit in each group, and it would be difficult to fit each of the English deists of the day neatly into one of Clarke's categories. It seems that his goal was not so much to develop a rubric for identifying how far each deist strayed from the truth of the gospel, but rather to call forward some of the important challenges that the English deists were raising against Christian belief. As such, each 'group' represents a specific challenge that the deist movement raised against orthodox Christianity.

In this context, then, it should be emphasized that the hallmark of Clarke's fourth group was probably the most important defining characteristic of the movement. The English deists believed in the method of natural religion, and reasonableness became a more important criterion for religious truthfulness than revelation. It was because of this methodological change that the English deists raised the theological questions which are characteristic of this age: questions regarding providence and the immortality of the soul, the relationship of ethics and religion, the status and necessity of the clergy, biblical criticism and the exclusivity of Christianity. What Clarke's analysis does provide is a nice introduction into the complexity of the questions raised by the English deists and also a flavor of the diversity of opinion that exists together under the rather unwieldy umbrella known as English deism.

One reason why it is so difficult to get a clear apprehension of what English deism entailed is the complexity of the intellectual debates of the period in question. This rigor is particularly true of the theological disagreements. That it was an amazingly rich and diverse intellectual age is apparent just from a list of some of the *major* thinkers who lived and wrote during the second half of the 17th century and the first half of the 18th: Thomas Hobbes, Robert Boyle, John Locke, Isaac Newton, Gottfried Leibniz, Jonathan Swift, George Berkeley, John Wesley Voltaire and, of course, David Hume. To this list should be added these names of men who were very influential in their day, but are less well known today, including: Joseph Butler, Samuel Clarke, John Wilkins, Francis Hutcheson and John Tillotson.[19]

It was a time when Newton's discoveries concerning the scientific laws of the universe were racing through the intellectual community and leaving profound effects on philosophy and theology, as can be witnessed in the examples of Locke and Clarke, respectively. Politically, it was a time in Great Britain when the Tory and Whig parties were emerging, each with different perspectives on the proper relationship between the monarchy and Parliament. Religiously, the scene was even more complicated. In addition to the ever-present Catholic/Protestant debates were these internal Protestant factions and groups: Anglicans and Dissenters, High-Church and Low-Church, orthodox and liberal, Quakers, Methodists, Latitudinarians, Levellers, Puritans, free-thinkers, Socinians and many more.

From this mix emerged the English deists, who engaged the intellectual discussions on several fronts. It is impossible to simply string all these positions out along a line or spectrum (left versus right or conservative against liberal), because the reality is that the debates and controversies operated on many levels. It is not uncommon to observe individuals, for instance, who disagreed with each another theologically, but agreed politically, or to see debates which range over a number of disciplines in complex ways. A few examples are in order.

One of the ongoing debates of the 17th century was the *rule of faith* controversy, in which Catholics asserted the certainty of their religious beliefs on the authority of the Church, while Protestants contended that religious certainty was to be found only in the Bible. The specific question at hand – on what basis is certainty acquired – proved to be relevant to a number of other debates. It soon migrated from the religious realm to the scientific with the formation of the Royal Society and its discussions of the foundations that Newtonian science provided for a more certain understanding of the universe. Eventually, this same language of certainty appeared in the writings of philosophical empiricists like Locke and Berkeley, as they wrestled with the question of certainty of knowledge.[20]

This debate is relevant to deism, because the more liberal Anglican theologians (known historically as the Latitudinarians) asserted that absolute certitude in matters theological rested only with God, but that Christianity could still be shown to be *reasonable*, that is, certain enough, to demand intellectual assent to its essential truthfulness. John Locke's *The Reasonableness of Christianity* (1695) makes just this point. English deists, like Locke's acquaintance, John Toland, who professed to be his disciple (much to Locke's chagrin), published just a year later his book entitled *Christianity not Mysterious*, in which a subtle, but very important shift can be detected. Locke argues that Christianity, known to be certainly true on the basis of divine revelation, also meets the requirements of reason. Christianity, for Locke, is doubly vindicated. For Toland, Christianity is not true until it has been shown to contain no mysteries which cannot be shown to be true by the light of natural reason. Christianity is only true insofar as it is shown to accord with natural religion. This position, that even direct revelation must meet the criterion of reasonableness in order to be held true, is elaborated on by various English deists and is one of the fundamental characteristics of the movement.

Another feature of the intellectual complexity of the era which mitigates against the rather simplistic theist/deist/atheist schema of Gaskin is the diversity among British Protestants. On one hand are the conservative, orthodox believers who affirm the traditional conception of God, believe the Bible records true history, and accept miracles and prophecies as divinely providential. This group is not homogeneous, as it includes Puritans, Quakers and Methodists and also individuals as diverse as Isaac Newton, George Berkeley and John Wesley. Distinct from these conservatives, on the other hand, are the more liberal churchmen who are often described in the literature as *rationalists* (not to be confused with Cartesian epistemologists), due to their tendency to emphasize and describe their faith in intellectual terms. Locke, Clarke, Butler, as well as the Latitudinarians, are examples of this perspective, but here as well, the rationalists were not monolithic, as Clarke tended towards Unitarianism, while Butler adhered to traditional Trinitarianism.

One of the forgotten aspects of this debate is that the theological rationalists were ardent believers in miracles *and* Newtonian science. In an important work *The Great Debate on Miracles*, Robert Burns contends that it was the apologetic program of the theological rationalists, which heavily stressed miracles, that provoked the English deist attack on miracles (among other things). Meanwhile, orthodox Christians (despite their belief in miracles) expressed some disquiet about the evidential *means* by which miracles were defended by the apologetic rationalists.[21]

The English deists inhabit still another point of view, in that they are inclined to reject miracles, to subject the Bible to intense criticism, to argue against the exclusivity of Christianity, to rail against the priesthood, and, most importantly, to accept Christianity only insofar as it is vindicated by natural religion. All of these positions made the orthodox Christians and the Latitudinarians uneasy, but for different reasons. The Latitudinarians and the English deists both employed some of the same rationalistic methods, but arrived at different conclusions. Some English deists agreed with the more conservative Christians on the immortality of the soul and the life to come, but offended the orthodox with their denigration of divine revelation. From still other perspectives are the skeptics like Hobbes and Spinoza, and closet atheists who may or may not have existed at this point of history.

Part of the complexity of this era stems from the fact that lines of disagreement were not always drawn in terms of left versus right or liberal against conservative. In actuality, it is not uncommon to find alliances or disagreements among various parties operating on more than one front. When the conservative divine James Foster took issue with Matthew Tindal's dismissal of miracles in *Christianity as Old as the Creation*, he also critiqued Samuel Clarke for his overly evidentialist and rationalist defense of the miraculous. Thus, Foster opens up two lines of battle, one against the English deists and one against the apologetic rationalists.[22]

In the fourth dialogue of *Alciphron*, Berkeley's interlocutors reflect this complexity. After Euphranor attempts to convince the free-thinking Alciphron of the existence of God, the other interlocutors, Crito and

Lysicles (despite being theists), debate the merits of Euphranor's rationalist account.[23] Shifting alliances between interlocutors is a dynamic mirrored in Hume's *Dialogues*. The prominent bishop of Bristol, Joseph Butler, wrote his famous *Analogy of Religion* to challenge the free-thinking ideas of English deists like Anthony Collins and Matthew Tindal. However, he is also well-known for forbidding Methodist evangelist John Wesley from preaching in his diocese, believing that the charismatic gifts of the Holy Spirit that were encouraged by Wesley, were, being nothing more than 'enthusiasms', a horror as bad as free-thinking.[24] Hume, as will be shown, occupies a unique position in these debates. He is skeptical, but not atheistic. He is opposed to miracles and enthusiasms, but is not an English deist. He weighs in on religious questions, but not from the perspective of revealed theology, but rather of philosophy.

The Agenda of English Deism

What did an English deist believe and how could one be identified as such? One simple definition is that deism is the Enlightenment philosophy of religion.[25] While it is true that English deism represents an application of the Enlightenment's beloved Reason to the issues of religion, this definition is too simple to be sufficient by itself. What needs to be recognized is that English deism is, first of all, a historical and theological movement which swirled around a collection of ideas, rather then a fixed system of doctrines. It resembles much more an *agenda* than a doctrinal statement of set positions. It bears, perhaps, a passing resemblance to movements like the current postmodernism or the scholasticism of the medieval era, in that these movements are characterized by the (sometimes contradictory) thoughts of a group of key individuals. If each of these three movements has an identity, it is because they inhabit a particular time and circumstance, and each member of the group is concerned about the same sorts of issues, even if they do not agree with each other on every particular.

Henning Graf Reventlow combines the insights of Ernst Troeltsch and Gunter Gawlick (both leading German scholars of English deism) and offers this description of what historical deism was:

According to the phrase of E. Troeltsch's which has become famous, Deism is the 'Enlightenment philosophy of religion.' Deism and Deist 'were originally self-designations of those who stood by the confession of natural religion (without always challenging the possibility of faith in revelation)'. It was 'the conviction of the Deists that there is a natural religion and that this precedes all religions of revelation . . . in it they saw contained the objective conditions of the good pleasure which God can take in men. They therefore declared that it was sufficient, and that to follow the precepts of natural religion, which together and individually had moral character, qualified a man for eternal salvation.'[26]

The primary characteristic of the English deists is that they held that the true religion is natural religion. Christianity is true only to the degree that it reflected the truth of nature.

This point can be clearly established by merely examining the *titles* of two of the mainstays of English deism. John Toland announced his position that Christianity is true because there is nothing in it that is beyond reason. It is *Christianity not Mysterious* – a religion that is entirely discursive and never inscrutable. The full title of what has been described as the 'bible' of English deism is Matthew Tindal's *Christianity as old as the Creation: or, The Gospel, a Republication of the Religion of Nature* (1730). For Tindal, Christianity only serves to repeat what is already discoverable in natural religion. Both Tindal and Toland were in agreement that primary locus of religious truth was found in nature, and what could be learned from natural religion was sufficient to discharge the religious duties of man.

Despite this rather philosophical main premise, the English deists engaged primarily in theological debate. Since their main concerns were theological, the English deists operated from within the broad confines of Christianity, not from without. Many of the different factions of the era (including progressives, conservatives and deists) were interested in establishing the rationality of the Christian religion. The theological character of the major disputes of the era is evident in this brief summary offered by Hefelbower:

> The main points in these discussions were the relation of reason and revelation, the truth and authority of revelation and scripture, the fact and evidential value of miracles, and the importance and authority of natural religion when compared with positive or revealed religion.[27]

Ronald Stromberg, while noting that it is impossible to give an exact picture of the theological beliefs which applied without qualification to all English deists, nevertheless, takes his readers on an 'imaginative tour of the mind of a typical deist'. Here, then, are some of the main stops on Stromberg's tour.[28] The English deists were much impressed by the discoveries of Newton, and the existence of immutable laws by which the universe operated led to their conclusion that religion must be rational. Unlike later generations of scientists, however, the English deists were not atheistic and did not see any conflict between science and religion. In this point of view, they agreed with the theological rationalists like Clarke and Butler. Their God was the supreme creator, and endowed with the great divine attributes of power, intelligence, infinitude and (sometimes) goodness. What bothered the English deists (and distanced them from the rationalists and the conservatives) was reconciling this Supreme Being with the God of the Old Testament who wrestled with Jacob, performed miracles, instituted a priesthood and revealed himself only to a small tribe of people, while purportedly ignoring the rest of the world.

The English deists were more impressed by the moral teachings of Jesus, but asserted that these same principles of morality were discoverable in nature and, in fact, existed in other cultures, like China and the Muslim countries. For the deists, the most important element of religion was its ethical component, and they tended to reduce religion to ethics. In fact, those elements of religious observance that went beyond ethics and morals were labeled *enthusiasms* (for example, the sacraments and other elements of worship). Nearly all English deists were unified in their ringing condemnations of *priestcraft*, historical and contemporary, and they spoke in very strident terms about the corruption that the priests wrought to the pure religion of nature by adding these cultic elements.

Following Hobbes, the English deists also engaged in higher criticism of the Bible, casting doubt on the veracity of the text of Scripture: its miracles and prophecies, its anthropomorphic descriptions of God and its exclusive claims regarding truth and salvation. Along the way, the English deists actively debated the existence of an immortal soul and the likelihood of future rewards and punishments in a life to come. Some asserted that reason taught that there must be a reckoning to come, since otherwise ethics in this life is futile, while others dismissed a future state altogether.

A list, then, of the important items on the agenda of the English deists would certainly contain the following items, organized by positions which they asserted, those which they contested, and those which they debated.

Positions asserted:

1. The best path to religious truth is found through nature and nature's religion.
2. Christianity (and other religions) is true to the degree to which it adheres to natural religion. Biblical revelation is, at best, a republication of the truth already available in nature.
3. God's existence is clearly evident through nature.

4. Nature also reveals to mankind what is truth of the nature of God.
5. Religion's most important contribution to mankind is in ethics, so that religion often reduces to ethics.

Positions contested:

6. The necessity of the priestcraft is questioned. Since it obscures the truth of natural religion, the priestcraft should be jettisoned.
7. The historicity of the Bible is suspect, due to many factors: miracles and prophecies, religious rituals, historical problems, etc. Biblical higher criticism is, thus, an important and necessary part of bringing Christianity up to the standards of natural religion.
8. The Judeo-Christian tradition has not been the exclusive, historical vessel of religious truth. Other historical religions (like Islam and Chinese religions) have also expressed the truth of natural religion, and have often done so much better than the Judeo-Christian tradition, particularly Judaism and Catholicism.

Positions debated:

9. The degree to which God exercises providence in the world is debatable.
10. The goodness of God is suspect to some thinkers.
11. The question of immortal souls and an afterlife is debatable.
12. Reports of miracles and prophecies in the Bible and in church history need to be examined.

The English Deists: A Brief Overview

This chapter is not intended to be a thorough explication of all the intricacies of the English deistic period, but rather to show that Hume is not a deist. Therefore, I will offer an overview of the representative teachings of the most important English deists in order to vindicate my summary of the movement above and also to provide a foil for Hume's own beliefs and methods.

The first noteworthy figure in the history of English deism is *Lord Herbert of Cherbury* (1581–1648), who actually significantly predates the era in question. Despite a gap of approximately 50 years between Cherbury's major publications and the next substantial contributions, and the fact that Cherbury was always a bit of an obscure thinker, his thoughts and conclusions anticipate nearly all of the English deist agenda. Nearly all historians recognize him as the precursor or father of English deism. His most famous book is *De Veritate*, first published in 1624, and in it, Cherbury develops five common notions (*notitiae communes*) which he believes are found implicit in the religious belief systems of all people. The importance of these common notions is categorically affirmed by Cherbury, which clearly articulates the supremacy of natural religion over written revelation:

> Every religion which proclaims a revelation is not good, nor is every doctrine which is taught under its authority always essential or even valuable. Some doctrines due to revelation may be, some of them ought to be, abandoned. In this connection the teaching of Common Notions is important; indeed, without them it is impossible to establish any standard of discrimination in revelation or even in religion.[29]

The five common notions are as follows. (1) 'There is a Supreme God', who is recognized by all religions. God is (according to Cherbury): blessed, the end towards which all things move, the cause of all things, the means by which all things are produced, eternal, good, just, wise, infinite, omnipotent and supremely free.[30] (2) 'This Sovereign Deity ought to be Worshipped', on the basis of the exercise of providential divine power. (3) 'The connection of Virtue with Piety, defined in this work as the right conformation of the faculties, is and always has been held to be, the most important part of religious practice.' Reventlow contends that this is the most important of the common notions for Cherbury, since it establishes the link between natural religion and ethics.[31] (4) 'The minds of men have always been filled with horror for their wickedness. Their vices and crimes have been obvious to them. They must be expiated by repentance.' Cherbury dismisses all the individual rites and sacrifices of the various religions, since they are not in general agreement. What he does assert, however, is that without genuine penitence which results in divine forgiveness, there is no way for man to obtain relief from the dreadful crush of sin. Thus, God would have created man only to punish him. This conclusion, according to Cherbury, is untenable.[32] (5) 'There is Reward or Punishment after this life.'

The common notions comprise Cherbury's positive teaching, but his deism has some negative elements. He opposed the Calvinist notions of original sin and predestination. He expressed repeated contempt for the priesthood for its imposition of irrational rites and sacrifices on the people, thus obscuring the rationality of natural religion. He was also a forerunner of the biblical criticism that was to become a characteristic of the more theologically skeptical age that followed him.[33] What makes Cherbury the forerunner of English deism is not solely the assertions of his common notions, but the fact that he defends their veracity solely on the basis of the authority of natural reason. His beliefs (both positive and negative) do link him with the English deists to come, although few follow him point-for-point on his common notions. What the other English deists did follow was Cherbury's method of developing and defending theological beliefs solely on the basis of natural reason, and they generally worked within the parameters of the agenda that Cherbury announced.

The next English deist of note is *Charles Blount* (1654–1693), an unfortunate figure in the history of the movement, who, despite generally recognized academic talents, borrowed so much from other writers that he has been named a plagiarizer.[34] In addition, he cut his career short by committing suicide over the impermissibility of marrying his dead wife's sister.[35] In his pamphlets, Blount reiterates Cherbury's five common notions, reworking them into seven articles. He also follows Cherbury in railing against the superstitions and ceremonies of the priestcraft and in stressing the ethical content of religion. He similarly believed that the immortality of the soul was a truth discoverable by natural religion.

A friend of Hobbes, Blount was a strident participant in the growing field of biblical criticism. His works were much more widely disseminated in Britain than were those of Cherbury, and the wide-ranging public debate on the agenda of the English deists can be traced to him. One of his books, an edition of Philostratus' *Life of Apollonius*, compared the miracles of Christ to an ancient, pagan miracle-worker named Apollonius. The effect was to ridicule Jesus by undermining the uniqueness of his miraculous powers. In the ensuing uproar, it was alleged that Blount's book was the most dangerous attack levied against revealed religion in his century, quite a charge indeed considering the fact that he shared the century with Hobbes and Spinoza.[36]

Another colorful English deist was *John Toland* (1670–1723), who managed to live just on the very edge of the intellectual community. Sir Leslie Stephen had a very low opinion of Toland, describing him as 'a mere waif and stray, hanging loose upon society, retiring at intervals into the profoundest recesses of Grub Street, emerging again by fits to scandalize the whole respectable world, and then once more sinking back into tenfold obscurity.'[37] Irish Catholic by birth, he converted to Protestantism and eventually published a book called *Pantheisticon* (1721), in which he espoused heretical pantheistic views. His already-mentioned *Christianity not Mysterious* (1696), however, was one of the signal deist works.

The brief first part ('Of Reason') reveals his indebtedness to Locke's empirical epistemology, as opposed to Cherbury's more Cartesian reliance on innate ideas. Despite the difference in epistemology, however, Toland endorsed the content of Cherbury's common notions. The second part of *Christianity not Mysterious* explores the heart of Toland's thesis, namely, 'That the Doctrines of the Gospel are not contrary to Reason'.

> But if we believe the *Scripture* to be Divine, not upon its own bare Assertion, but from a real Testimony consisting in the Evidence of the things contain'd therein; from undoubted Effects, and not from Words and Letters; what is this but to prove it by *Reason?* It has in it self, I grant, the brightest Characters of *Divinity:* But 'tis Reason finds them out, examines them, and by its Principles approves and pronounces them sufficient; which orderly begets in us an Acquiescence of *Faith* or Perswasion.[38]

According to Toland, the miracles of the Bible (once they are explained scientifically) reveal that Christianity was indeed intended to be a rational and intelligible religion, since they show Christ to have authority. He does not address the conclusion of some English deists that the very notion of a miracle is an irrational one.

The last section of *Christianity not Mysterious* addresses Toland's theological concern that Paul (and other biblical writers) endorses mysteries in the faith. Part of the answer for Toland is that the New Testament is given to reveal mysteries not known prior to this time, and the other part is that these things were mysteries in the first part only because of the obscurantism of the priests.[39] The underlying thesis of Toland's work is that whatever can be known cannot be mysterious. Since Christianity and Christianity's God can be known, they cannot be mysterious. The result is a religion that is both rational and Christian.

Anthony Ashley Cooper, the Third Earl of Shaftesbury (1671–1713) is often mentioned with the English deists, and his best-known work, *Characteristicks of Men, Manner, Opinion, Times* (1711) was one of the most widely printed books of the era. Although Shaftesbury shares some of the deist agenda, he is at least equally influenced by Stoic philosophy and the ideals of Renaissance humanism. His overriding concern was to establish a system of morality based on an innate moral sense, and his conclusion was that neither a god nor religion was necessary for developing virtue.[40] Shaftesbury was not an atheist, but he did not write from within the contexts of Christian theology, as did, for example, Toland. He is less interested in establishing the truthfulness of natural religion, which means that he is not necessarily properly understood as an English deist, although he does reject miracles and engages in some biblical criticism.[41]

One of the more prominent English deists was the self-styled 'free-thinker' *Anthony Collins* (1676–1729), whose book *A Discourse of Free-Thinking* (1713) is one of the major publications of English deism. Acquainted with Locke[42] and influenced by his ideas on toleration, Collins' main thesis is that the entirely free exercise of human reason is needed in order to discover truth. He is particularly critical of the clergy who insist on true belief over free thought. He expresses his basic contention in the following way:

> If the surest and best means of arriving at Truth lies in *Free-Thinking*, then the whole Duty of Man with respect to Opinions lies only in *Free-Thinking*. Because he who *thinks freely* does his best towards being in the right, and consequently does all that God, who can require nothing more of any Man than that he should do his best, can require of him. . . . On the other side, the whole Crime of Man, with respect to Opinions, must lie in his not *thinking freely*.[43]

Collins goes on to assert that it is by free-thinking that one may know God and all of his perfect attributes, and live his life in perfect peace and happiness, while all the religious rituals and other requirements of the priests can never make a person more acceptable to God.

At the end of the *Discourse on Free-Thinking*, Collins makes a list of notable free-thinkers in history who should serve as example. The list is an intriguing one, including prominent pagan philosophers like Socrates, Plato, Aristotle and Cicero, but also some members of the Judeo-Christian tradition (Solomon, the Jewish prophets, Josephus and Origen), plus more contemporary figures like Bacon, Hobbes and Tillotson. What the list suggests is that Collins does not think that Christianity and free-thinking are mutually exclusive, although there is much in the Christian tradition that needs correcting. Collins is critical of the Bible since it fosters different interpretations and leads to contradictory sects and traditions. He believes that the text itself has, due to the influence of the priests, become unreliable, and, thus, has grave reservations about literal interpretation of the Bible.[44] Despite the extremely critical nature of his comments on Christianity and the Bible, Collins remained a practicing member of the church until his death.[45]

A unique and charming figure in the history of English deism was *William Wollaston* (1659–1724), a London clergyman, who, after inheriting a large sum of money, retired and spent thirty years thinking about the problem of natural religion. The result was a book entitled *Religion of Nature Delineated* (1722), which was widely read and quoted during the first half of the 18th century. Hume occasionally alluded to and critiqued this work in his *Treatise* and the first *Enquiry*, particularly with regard to the foundations of ethics (cf. T 2.1.7.2) and notions of chance and probability (cf. EHU Section 6). Wollaston's primary goal was to establish a system of morality derived entirely from reason. He is not always considered among the deists, since his work lacks the vitriol characteristic of most English deists, and because of his fairly orthodox conclusions. He affirms the immateriality and immortality of the soul, as well as an afterlife in which rewards and punishment are handed down. He also held to a particular providence and the efficacy of prayer. Wollaston, however, should be viewed as an English deist, because he based his theological system squarely on natural religion and almost not at all on the Bible.[46]

The last great work of the English deists is *Christianity as old as the Creation*1730) by *Matthew Tindal* (1657–1733). As a champion of natural religion, Tindal functions as an apologist for both Christianity and natural religion.[47] Tindal holds that Christianity is a duplication of the truth already made available to all people through reason. It is through reason that we know that God is perfect and what our duty to him is. Since God is immutable and the duties of the natural law are also unchanging, then it is clear that a religion that is rooted in history and with a particular people cannot be the truth, unless, of course, the historical religion is subordinate to an already-established natural religion. It is this project that Tindal takes pains to show. The seeming contradictions between natural religion (as the English deists describe it) and Christianity can be reconciled by the methods of biblical criticism and a removal of the enthusiasms introduced into Christianity by the corrupting influences of priestcraft.

> In a word, there's nothing in itself so indifferent, either as to matter or manner; but if it be engrafted into Religion and monopoliz'd by the Priests, may endanger the substance of it: This has been plainly shewn by those Divines, who, at the *Reformation*, & since, have argu'd against all impositions; they have prov'd that most of the corruptions of *Popery* began at some Rites, which seem'd at first very innocent; but were afterwards abus'd to Superstition and Idolatry, and swell'd up to that bulk, as to oppress, and stifle True Religion with their Number and Weight.[48]

Thus, Tindal, like the other English deists, formulates his religion on the basis of the light of reason. A divine being exists and is possessed of great attributes. He creates the universe and a natural law, by which humans may know right from wrong and worship the creator. The enthusiasms fostered by the priesthood together with the miracles and other problems of the Bible obscure the connection that rightfully exist between the religion of nature and the religion of Christ. Tindal, like Toland and Collins, works specifically from within the bounds of theology to show that Christianity can be made to meet the criterion of reason.

Ultimately, however, as a movement, English deism failed. There was no organized school of deist thought in Britain. There were too many dis-agreements, and too little first class scholarship. They were drowned in a sea of protest, some of it scholarly and some of it rhetorical. The last of the English deists, men like Thomas Chubb and Thomas Morgan and Peter Annet, carried on the debate for some time, but after 1740, the deists faded from the intellectual scene, at least in Britain, and this era draws to a close. David Hume, who came of age in the midst of these debates, witnessed the demise of English deism. The question to consider is whether he was one of their number or whether he was one among the chorus that engulfed them out.

Was Hume an English Deist?

In order to address this question of Hume's relation to English deism, it is only fair to consider the reasons for thinking him to be one. There are really only two reasons to link him with English deism. The first one is that Hume does agree with the English deist agenda on a number of significant points, and the second (which grows out of the first) is that Hume's con-temporaries sometimes named him among the deists. The first reason is the most substantial, and so it is appropriate to review the positions that Hume holds in common with the English deists. Hume famously argues against the possibility of there ever being sufficient testimony to justify one's belief in a purported miracle. He is skeptical that there is a future life to come or that humans possess an immortal soul. He is a frequent critic of enthusi-asms, and he has some grave doubts about the degree to which God may be said to exercise providence over the world.[49]

To make the case that Hume is not part of the movement of English deism, it is necessary to address these issues. The first point in my conten-tion that Hume was not an English deist is the recognition that agreement with some of the beliefs of a particular group does not suggest, without fail, that one is to be identified with that group. A person is not a Republican or a Christian or a Platonist just because there are some beliefs the individual shares with the group in question. What needs to be examined is whether one holds to the core, essential beliefs of that group or holds a vast majority of the beliefs of that group or whether one names himself a member of that group. Minus any of these coherences, that individual cannot be identified by the moniker of that group.

In America, one is likely to be a Democrat or a Republican since we live (largely) in a two-party system. Thus, it is likely that someone who believes in smaller government and argues for tax reduction is a Republican, although possibly a Libertarian. The situation, however, was not so straight-forward in the 18th century Great Britain. The multiplicity of theological positions and the complexity of the debates meant that matching an indi-vidual with one of the parties in the discussion was often difficult. One could side with the Latitudinarians on one question, the deists on another, the conservatives on still another issue, while not specifically identifying with *any* group.

This state of affairs is particularly true with Hume, especially when one recalls what a unique and iconoclastic thinker he was. One of the reasons that Hume was called a deist was that he agreed with some of their beliefs, but did not have confidence in the enterprise of natural religion to the degree that the English deists did. Put another way, Hume did not adhere to the core premise of English deism, namely, that natural religion was the best path to religious truth, nor did he hold an overwhelming majority of the characteristic positions of English deism, nor did he allow himself to be called a deist. Thus, while Hume may be sympathetic with some of the English deists who argued against the historicity of biblical miracles, this fact does not make him an English deist, rather only a participant in the wide-ranging and complex theological debates of the 18th century Britain.

Hume addresses this problem very explicitly in *A Letter from a Gentleman to His Friend in Edinburgh*, which he composed after being denied the position of chair of Ethics and Pneumatic Philosophy at the University of Edinburgh. In the *Letter*, he lists the various extreme positions and false conclusions which are attributed to him by those unable to understand either the sub-tlety of his own thought or his relationship to the complex intellectual scene. He specifically addresses the most important distinction between himself and the English deists:

In Reality, whence come all the various Tribes of Hereticks, the *Arians, Socinians* and *Deists*, but from too great a Confidence in mere human Reason, which they regard as the *Standard* of every Thing, and which they will not submit to the superior Light of Revelation? And can one do a more essential Service to Piety, than by showing them that this boasted Reason of theirs, so far from accounting for the great Mysteries of the Trinity and Incarnation, is not able fully to satisfy itself with regard to its own Operations, and must in some Measure fall into a Kind of implicite Faith, even in the most obvious and familiar Principles? (LG 21)

Although many commentators are tempted to see Hume speaking somewhat disingenuously here in his efforts to defend orthodox Christian beliefs, it is better to see Hume situating himself within the complex theological arena of his times. He does not agree with the English deists and others who hold such a strong view of human reason that even revelation needs to measure up to it. As a result of pointing out the fallibility of human reason in the *Treatise*, Hume is doing a service to those orthodox Christians who wish to preserve the mysteries of their faith, even if they are above reason. Hume does not share all their religious beliefs, but that is not the point at hand. He does agree with the fideists (against the deists) that human reason is fallible, a position that is in keeping with his mitigated skepticism. Again, agreement or disagreement with one or both groups on a specific point does not necessitate identification with either group.

Secondly, Hume did not hold to their major premise that reason was an infallible guide to religious truth. For Hume, religious beliefs grow out of our human nature and the natural dispositions that we each possess. In an overlooked article that contrasts Hume's methods with leading English deists, like Toland, Collins and Tindal, James O'Higgins nicely summarizes this important distinction:

Religion [for Hume] was not the product of reason but of sentiment and the passions. Its origin was the propensity to believe in 'invisible, intelligent power'. And this propensity, which he describes as universal or almost universal, is a basic fact of human nature. . . . Religion was, in other words, not a product of ratiocination. It corresponded to something other in human nature.[50]

The propensities that O'Higgins mentions are a continual theme in Hume's *Natural History*, in which Hume argues that our religious beliefs are not the product of argumentation or demonstration, but an innate inclination that has more to do with our fixed human nature than discursive thought. These propensities are sometimes contradictory, as when wonders lead us to worship a majestic deity, but terrors lead us to fear evil gods (NHR 13.3).

Sometimes we try to link our propensities to our impressions and ideas, which leads to things like polytheism or idolatry (NHR 5.2):

> The universal propensity to believe in invisible, intelligent power, if not an original instinct, being at least a general attendant of human nature, may be considered as a kind of mark or stamp, which the divine workman has set upon his work; and nothing surely can more dignify mankind, than to be thus selected from all other parts of the creation, and to bear the image or impression of the universal Creator. (NHR 15.5)

The analysis of these propensities and the ways that they have played out in the history of religious expression makes up the bulk of the *Natural History*, which is markedly different in tone and content from deistic works like Tindal's *Christianity as old as Creation*. Tindal and the English deists focused on showing that God exists through argumentation and attempted to prove that the basic truths of natural religion were shared by all religions. Hume does not argue for the existence of God the way that the English deists do, although (as I will show in Chapter 4) he does see evidence for the existence of God in the world. The difference between Hume and the English deists, however, is the degree of confidence that they put in the role of reason. Hume has a relatively low level of confidence in reason, but allows that people are so constructed as to assert the existence of the deity, but in various ways: polytheistic and monotheistic, sophisticated and unsophisticated and so on. The English deists, on the other hand, based their entire system on the successfulness of the enterprise of natural theology.

A third reason that Hume is not an English deist is that he does not write from within the Christian tradition like they do. Nearly all of the English deists (Cherbury, Toland, Tindal, Wollaston and, to a degree, Collins) manage to maintain the rather incongruous combination of supposing Christianity to be secondary to natural religion, while still operating from within a theological point of view. Hume's method is otherwise. Although he is interested in questions of religion, he does not critique the miracles of the Bible by doing biblical criticism. He does so by challenging the way one must view the veracity of the testimony regarding miracles. Hume is a philosopher and only investigates religious questions with the tools that philosophy provides. In doing so, he shows himself not to be an English deist.

A fourth difference is that Hume does not agree with the English deists on the question of religion and ethics. The English deists believed (generally speaking) that the primary importance of religion was its moral teaching. They held this belief so strongly that they tended to reduce religion simply to ethics and sought to eliminate the ritual and sacramental aspects of religion. Hume famously believed that religion (at least, false religion) was an impediment to ethics, and that religion was not necessary for a proper understanding of ethical theory and moral responsibilities. Hume's works on ethics were scandalous to some of his contemporaries because he did not defer to a religious basis for morality, nor did he hold that ethics helped prepare the way for natural religion. The former was a problem for the religiously orthodox, while the latter was contrary to the point of view of the English deists. Hume's disdain for 'monkish virtues' in a famous passage from the second *Enquiry* shows his distance from both conservative Christians and English deists who saw ethics as a way to worship God (EPM 9.1.3). With regard to ethical theory, the English deists tend to be natural lawyers, which is consistent with their emphasis on natural religion. One of the truths that they glean from nature is the ethical law which God has written into it. Hume does not hold to a natural law, but bases his ethical theory on the development of the proper human sentiments in the passions.

Still another difference that can be drawn between Hume and the English deists (the fifth reason) is their attitudes towards the priesthood. The deists of Hume's day were generally uniform in their strident castigation of the clergy. They blamed the priests for the corruption of the purity of natural religion and for the enthusiasms and superstitions of religious practice. Hume also often writes against enthusiasms and superstitions, but he tends to blame the 'vulgar' (common, uneducated people) for such abuses. In the essay 'On Superstition and Enthusiasms', he does hold the priests responsible for superstitions, but not enthusiasms, which tend to arise from the laity. Although Hume does note priestly abuses in the *Natural History*, his general thesis is that the abuses in popular religion are due to the weaknesses present universally in all humans and not just the clergy. Thus, his criticisms of the priesthood are, in general, much more moderate than those of the major English deists, although, it must be admitted that this distinction is one of degree rather than kind.

This moderation suggests a sixth difference between Hume and the English deists. Hume was part of the intellectual establishment. His writings were polished, widely read and an important contributing factor to the Scottish Enlightenment. Hume aimed at the rather difficult ideal of becoming a well-respected and moderate public intellectual, while at the same time, taking on beliefs as divergent and cherished as miracles, a future state and causality. Mostly, Hume succeeded at being responsibly controversial, although his views did cost him a professorship at the University of Edinburgh and scandalized the most conservative Christians of his day. The English deists, however, never attained Hume's standing in society. Many of their writings tended to be pamphlets, heavy on the rhetoric and light on substance. Their few important works have never stood on their own as important contributions to the substance of human learning. They are important only because they best represent the brief chapter of English deism. The English deists lived on the outskirts of intellectual society. They founded no school, and excited much more opposition than agreement. In an era of many outstanding thinkers, the English deists were poor cousins, whose ideas aroused much debate, but ultimately were drowned out by the many voices of opposition, one of which was David Hume's.

Finally, the seventh reason that Hume is not an English deist is that he did not share their beliefs about God, although what Hume did actually think about the deity is a complicated matter, and one that I will take up in the next chapter. So, with all these differences between Hume and the English deists, it is reasonable to ask just why the 18th century authors like Philip Skelton[51] and John Leland[52] did identify Hume as a deist? The answer is straightforward. Both Skelton and Leland were conservative Christians who were threatened by the various heretical positions that were current in English thought. Their intentions were not to produce a careful historical analysis of the different positions that existed in England, but rather to expose theological error and to defend the orthodox faith. *Deism* was a term in flux at that time, sometimes used carefully to reflect those who relied solely on natural religion, but at other times as a term of abuse to anyone who espoused nonorthodox beliefs. That some contemporaries of Hume applied the term in this second sense to him does not carry much weight in light of the significant differences that existed between Hume and the English deists.[53]

Lastly, no account of Hume and English deism can be complete without recounting the charming story (as remembered by Lord Charlemont) of an exchange between Hume and a Mrs. David Mallet, especially since it revealed Hume's dislike for the term.

I never saw him so much displeased, or so much disconcerted as by the Petulance of Mrs. Mallet, the pert and conceited Wife of Bolingbroke's Editor. This lady, who was not acquainted with Hume, meeting him one night at an Assembly, boldly accosted him in these Words – 'Mr. Hume, Give me leave to introduce myself to you. We Deists ought to know one another.' – 'Madam,' replied He, 'I am no Deist. I do na style myself so, neither do I desire to be known by that Appellation.'[54]

Thus, I conclude that it is inaccurate to include Hume among the English deists of his day. In addition, since I have shown that popular deism is a term better suited for a later age, it follows that it is a mistake to name Hume a deist in either the popular or historical sense. The evidence for Hume's theism is the subject of the next chapter.

Chapter 4

Hume on the Existence of God

True Religion and Genuine Theism

Readers of David Hume are frequently struck by these two observations, first, that Hume is very critical of religion, and, second, that he cannot seem to stop writing and thinking about it. The simultaneous disdain and obsession with religion is sufficient to give his interpreters pause. If he is so contemptuous of religion, why does he not just dismiss it altogether in favor of other more promising topics for his fertile mind to investigate? One of two answers are usually given to this question. The first, and more frequent answer, is that Hume finds so much in religion that is bad and detrimental to society that he takes it as a civic duty to free humanity from the corrupting influences of the superstitions of religion. Thus, his passion for religion is the result of his overwhelming desire to see it soundly critiqued. An example of those who give this answer is Norman Kemp Smith:

> There is, indeed, little of the sceptical *inquirer* in Hume's writings on religion. Once he had succeeded in formulating the general lines of his own philosophy, he had quite definitely concluded that religion is not merely an ambiguous but in the main a *malign* influence. For Hume's own continuing personal difficulties were not in regard to this or that religious tenet, but in regard to religion itself: why, human life being what he took it to be, religion should exist at all; why religion, being preposterous in any form, should yet be so universally influential in so many different forms; and why in his own time it should be so widely prevalent in the grim and gloomy form of the Calvinist creed.[1]

This answer is not without merit. Hume was an unrepentant critic of the abuses and superstitions that he saw in organized religion, and is notorious for his strong critiques of several cherished religious convictions: miracles, a future life, a soul, the need for a religious foundation for ethics, among others. Even right up to the end of his life, Hume joked from his deathbed with Adam Smith that one of the few reasons he might offer for the need to prolong his life was, 'If I live a few years longer, I may have the satisfaction of seeing the downfall of some of the prevailing systems of superstition' (L.3 Appendix; 2.451).

My preference, however, is for a second answer to the question of why Hume was so preoccupied with religion. While it is certainly true that he saw much in religious devotion and observance that he wished to refute, it is my contention that he also desired to distinguish that which was true in religion from that which was false, vulgar and popular. His preoccupation with religion, then, stems from these two goals: initially, to critique the harmful effects of false religion, but, secondly, to identify what is true and proper in religion.

One tantalizing piece of evidence that suggests that Hume does see a positive role for religion in society comes from his essay entitled 'Idea of a Perfect Commonwealth', which is an exercise somewhat akin to More's *Utopia*. What is interesting in Hume's hypothetical form of government, to which, he suggests, he cannot 'in theory, discover any considerable objection' (E IC, 516) is that he allows for 'a council for religion and learning' which oversees the universities and the clergy (E IC, 518–519), and he also defends the necessity of the clergy (E IC, 525).

Admittedly, finding legitimate religious beliefs occupied far less of Hume's attention than castigating illegitimate ones, but it is nevertheless accurate that on numerous occasions, Hume describes what he calls *true religion* and *genuine theism*. It is a disservice to his thought that these passages are often ignored or marginalized. For instance, Mossner concludes that Hume rejected all supernatural content in religion in favor of a completely naturalistic 'religion of man'. The upshot, Mossner counsels, is that the reader of Hume must recognize 'a sustained irony in Hume's every statement on religion'.[2]

Similarly, M. A. Box opines that 'while no one, perhaps, has yet been able to codify definitively what exactly it was that Hume called true religion, few readers have not been able to see through his ironic genuflexions.'[3] The task of codifying Hume's religious beliefs, which Box so blithely disregards, is precisely the goal of this chapter. It is my conclusion that Hume did believe that there was a true religion, built around a genuine theism. Further, I hold that uncovering this often overlooked part of Hume's philosophy of religion will help the readers of Hume to understand more fully his two most important works on religion: the *Natural History of Religion* and the *Dialogues concerning Natural Religion*. Articulating this true religion will also enable them to appreciate to a greater degree Hume's brooding fixation on religious matters, and to discern what Hume truly believed about the existence and nature of God.

'Of Superstition and Enthusiasm'

The essay entitled 'Of Superstition and Enthusiasm' was one of the original articles included in Hume's first collection of essays, published in 1741 as *Essays, Moral and Political*. Thus, this essay represents some of Hume's first published thoughts on religion (following the brief direct comments in the *Treatise*). It is, then, instructive to note that the very first sentence makes the distinction between true and false religion, as well as the further distinction that the two main species of false religion are *superstition* and *enthusiasm* (E SE, 73). Hume cites the maxim 'that the corruption of the best things produces the worst', thus implying that (true) religion, being one of the best things, can still produce the worst abuses, namely superstition and enthusiasm. This dichotomy anticipates the 'flux and reflux' theme of the cycles between monotheism and polytheism, which figures so prominently in the *Natural History*.

Hume makes an interesting distinction between these two species of false religions, which is carried over into all his writings on religion. Characteristic again of the future *Natural History*, he begins with an analysis of human nature. Given that the human mind is prone to 'certain unaccountable terrors and apprehensions' which are not entirely attributable to known objects, a person begins to fear unknown or imaginary horrors. These vague fears give rise to superstitions:

> As these enemies are entirely invisible and unknown, the methods taken to appease them are equally unaccountable, and consist in ceremonies, observances, mortifications, sacrifices, presents, or in any practice, however, absurd or frivolous, which either folly or knavery recommends to a blind and terrified credulity. Weakness, fear, melancholy, together with ignorance, are, therefore, the true sources of *Superstition*. (E SE, 74)

However, the human mind is not only prone to unknown fears, but also to 'unaccountable elevation and presumption' which greatly inflates the imagination, making all the things of this world seem unimportant and worthless, in favor of the wonders of the spiritual realm.

> Hence arise raptures, transports, and surprising flights of fancy; and confidence and presumption still encreasing, these raptures, being altogether

unaccountable, and seeming quite beyond the reach of our ordinary faculties, are attributable to the immediate inspiration of that Divine Being, who is the object of devotion. In a little time, the inspired person comes to regard himself as a distinguished favourite of the Divinity; and when this frenzy takes place, which is the summit of enthusiasm, every whimsy is consecrated. . . . Hope, pride, presumption, a warm imagination, together with ignorance, are, therefore, the true sources of *Enthusiasm.* (E ES, 74)

Superstitions and enthusiasms are opposites. They push away from the moderate middle (presumably where true religion is located) to find differing errors at the extremes. Hume provides some examples of these religious corruptions. The authority and predominance of priests is due to superstition, while Protestant sects like the Quakers and the Presbyterians bear the characteristics of enthusiasm. Another example comes from the 17th century French theological debate between the Molinists and the Jansenists. The Molinist movement (representing Jesuit teaching) was basically superstitious in its outlook, while Jansenists, like Pascal, reveal a tendency to enthusiasm. It is apparent that Hume sees superstition – more often associated with Catholicism and Judaism – as the more dangerous of the two extremes. Meanwhile, enthusiasm, which is more characteristic of Protestant Christianity, has some redeeming features in terms of mitigating some of the authoritarian excesses of superstition.

What is significant about Hume's treatment of superstition and enthusiasm is that he does not critique the phenomena simply by asserting that all religion is false and that all notions of the divine are fictitious from the start. Hume's analysis falls far short of that which is offered by later critics of religion such as Ludwig Feuerbach and Sigmund Freud, who argue that the notion of God is simply a contrived set of idealized human traits, and a psychological crutch with no basis in reality. Hume's comments about divinity in this essay do *not* imply that there is no such being, only that the religiously superstitious and the enthusiastic fanatic are mistaken in some of their beliefs regarding the deity. In this essay, Hume does not describe what true religion is, nor does he specifically assert the existence of God or endorse the right way to relate to him. What Hume does instead is criticize two excesses of religion without repudiating the entire enterprise.

Since the point that the excesses of false religion do not repudiate the entire enterprise of religion is consistent with the main purpose of the essay (to identify and distinguish these two phenomena of false religion), one can rule out irony here. Thus, the essay 'Of Superstition and Enthusiasm' serves as a helpful introduction into Hume's thoughts on religion, and it sets the stage for his major works in philosophy of religion.

Natural History of Religion: Two Stories

The long essay given the title 'The Natural History of Religion' was originally published as one of the *Four Dissertations* in 1757, although it is likely that Hume composed the *Natural History* at least six years earlier.[4] The *Four Dissertations* have a colorful history, since at one point, it was to include the eventually suppressed essays 'Of Suicide' and 'Of the Immortality of the Soul'. Word of Hume's arguments excited much controversy, and Hume ultimately opted not to issue the essays. The published version finally then included the *Natural History* as well as the essays 'Of the Passions', 'Of Tragedy' and 'Of the Standard of Taste'.

Despite the suppression of the two infamous essays, the *Four Dissertations* still attracted some criticism. One of the most prominent critics was the Reverend William Warburton, a frequent opponent of Hume's. In a letter to Hume's publisher, Warburton offers the following assessment of the *Natural History*.

> The design of the first essay [the *Natural History*] is the very same with all Lord Bolingbrooke's, to establish *naturalism*, a species of atheism, instead of religion; and he employs one of Bolingbrooke's capital arguments for it. All the difference is, it is without Bolingbrooke's abusive language. . . . He is establishing atheism; and in one single line of a long essay professed to believe Christianity.[5]

Other reviews were more judicious. One contemporary who concluded that Hume 'has finely exposed superstition and popery: professeth himself an advocate of pure theism: And so far as he is a theist, he cannot be an enemy to genuine christianity'.[6] This review reflects some of the themes that I will be exploring, and is more in keeping with my own interpretation of the *Natural History* over against Warburton's judgment.

In comparison with the *Treatise*, the *Dialogues* and even the first *Enquiry*, the *Natural History of Religion* has been, for the most part, under-explored by Hume scholars. There are no book-length studies of it, and the number of articles devoted wholly to it is small. One of the best recent treatments is an article entitled 'Hume's Project in "The Natural History of Religion"' by Lorne Falkenstein. One of the merits of Falkenstein's work is that he understands the *Natural History* within the context of the essay 'Of Superstition and Enthusiasm'. Since Hume characterizes the rise of both monotheism and polytheism as due to fear and ignorance, the implication is that the religion examined in the *Natural History* is predominantly superstition. As Falkenstein concludes, '"The natural history of religion" is really just a natural history of superstition.'[7]

However, Falkenstein's analysis is ultimately flawed in that he underestimates the importance of true religion in the *Natural History*. He notes that the introduction to the book affirms the rational basis for 'the primary principles of genuine Theism and Religion', but notes that the phrase *genuine theism* occurs only twice in Hume's writings – here and on the lips of Cleanthes in DNR 12.24. Consequently, Falkenstein dismisses the references to genuine theism as insincere concessions on Hume's part in order to focus attention on what Falkenstein presumes to be the primary point of the book, namely, to critique the superstition found in popular religion.[8]

Falkenstein argues that there are four ways to take Hume's repeated assertions regarding the references to genuine theism that are supported by the design argument. (1) The remarks are insincere and motivated by a desire to obfuscate his project. (2) The remarks are insincere, but motivated mainly by a desire to simply concede that point in order to focus on the critique of superstition. This conciliatory point of view is Falkenstein's position. (3) The remarks are sincere, but actually concede almost nothing about any legitimate religious belief. This Falkenstein takes to be Gaskin's position of attenuated deism. (4) The remarks are sincere and express some sort of significant religious commitment. This position is the one that I will defend. Falkenstein rejects it due to his continued adherence to the conventional story, and also because he holds that genuine theism must include some belief in the afterlife and a morally good god.

Falkenstein's analysis is erroneous on several points. First, Hume employs a number of equivalent phrases for *genuine theism* which Falkenstein ignores. He speaks of the *pure principles of theism* (NHR 1.5), *genuine theists* (NHR 4.1), *genuine principles of theism* (NHR 15.4), plus at least one other direct reference to genuine theism in NHR 7.3. The real point, however, is not to quibble over the number of times Hume uses a particular phrase, but to observe what he truly affirms. As I will show, it will be very untenable to hold Falkenstein's thesis that references to genuine theism are insincere concessions, because in fact, Hume is setting the stage for an important distinction between two kinds of religion, the true religion and the vulgar religion.[9] In fact, the major theme of the first half of the book is devoted to distinguishing between genuine theism and vulgar theism, and the clear indication is that

Hume affirms the former. This distinction begins obliquely in the very first sentence of the Introduction to the book:

> As every enquiry, which regards religion, is of the utmost importance, there are two questions in particular, which challenge our attention, to wit, that concerning its foundation in reason, and that concerning its origin in human nature. Happily, the first question, which is the most important, admits of the most obvious, at least, the clearest, solution. The whole frame of nature bespeaks an intelligent author; and no rational enquirer can, after serious reflection, suspend his belief a moment with regard to the primary principles of genuine Theism and Religion. (NHR Introduction)

Although Falkenstein and others see this passage as the height of irony, it is difficult to see how a text like this one, which opens a small treatise in which Hume speaks in his own voice, can be responsibly thought to be insincere, especially when he is introducing one of the main themes of the book. What is overlooked, I believe, is a level of complexity and nuance in Hume's thoughts on God and religion, which most Hume scholars are unwilling to acknowledge. In nearly every one of the first seven chapters, Hume articulates a distinction between these two conceptions of religion, and these two stories of the beginnings of religion are the major theme of the early chapters.

In the Introduction, Hume contends that our religious ideas are the results of certain *propensities* that are universal in all persons. It is these propensities (to fear or to exalt, for example) that lead to the idea of divine beings and spiritual convictions, and, ultimately, to the sorts of superstitions that Hume catalogues in the *Natural History* and roundly criticizes. The problem is reconciling this more psychological analysis of the beginning of religion with the discursive approach based on evidence of design, to which the Introduction alludes. It seems that Hume cannot have both arguments, which is why many commentators think that Hume is being ironic or less than sincere with regard to the first question. Either there really is a divine being, whose existence may be inferred rationally from 'the whole frame of nature' or else mankind invents the idea of god out of a need to come to grips with our natural propensities, but it seems unlikely that one person can endorse both perspectives.

I submit, however, that Hume *does* indeed retain both arguments, but only one of them reveals *genuine* theism. The whole of nature does reveal the true god, and this is true religion. False, vulgar and popular religion, however, arises from our human propensities, and it is precisely these forms of religion that need refutation.

One objection to the two-stories interpretation is that it necessitates that Hume accept some truths on the basis of natural religion. In fact, it is clear from what has been investigated thus far, that this contention is true. When Hume claims that 'the whole frame of nature bespeaks an intelligent author,' this proposition is clearly offered on the basis of natural theology. A tension arises, however, in that it was claimed that one of the key differences between Hume and the English deists was that Hume did not believe that reason was an infallible guide to religious truth, and thus he was critical of their pervasive natural theology. This distinction can still be maintained, even in light of Hume's belief in the existence of a deity on the basis of evidence found in nature, because Hume goes no further with natural theology than what it reveals about God. The key here is that Hume severely limits what can be known from natural theology, while the English deists, in general, believed that all the genuine truths of Christianity (and any other religion, for that matter) could be discovered through natural theology. The English deists ultimately erred (according to Hume), because they placed too much confidence in their reasoning abilities in matters theological, and they carried their natural religion too far. Put another way, the English deists held that the best way to discover theological truth was through reason applied to nature, and that this project can be so successfully completed that there is no need for special revelation. Hume does not have this degree of confidence in the project of natural theology, although he does allow that some truths regarding the deity can be observed.

In the first chapter, Hume develops a position that proved to be very contentious to the theologically conservative Christians of his day, namely, that polytheism was the original religious point of view of earliest mankind, and monotheism (being more sophisticated) only arose as the thought of men and women became correspondingly more refined and developed. This theory was scandalous to those well-versed in biblical history, since the book of Genesis indicates that God revealed himself to Adam, Noah and Abraham, and he taught them to worship him as the all-powerful and holy Creator of the world. Corruptions of this original monotheism only arose because of idolatry and lack of obedience to the law of God. Thus, the story of the Bible is the exact opposite of Hume's hypothesis that polytheism is the original religion of man, and that monotheism gradually emerges from it (or perhaps develops separately from it). It is this thesis that contemporaries like Warburton found so distasteful.[10] What is overlooked, however, is that Hume's analysis does not challenge the point of view that there is true religion and false religion. It only differs in the historical accounts of their beginnings.

Hume argues that it is just as silly to imagine that people lived in palaces before they built huts and cottages or that they developed geometry before discovering agriculture as it is to imagine that they asserted 'that the Deity appeared to them a pure spirit, omniscient, omnipotent and omnipresent, before he was apprehended to be a powerful, though limited being, with human passions and appetites, limbs and organs' (NHR 1.5). Hume's point was that the mind 'rises gradually'. It naturally progresses from inferior thoughts to superior, not the reverse. Thus, the more refined notions of a divine being possessing the perfections mentioned above can only develop over time.

> Nothing could disturb this natural progress of thought, but some obvious and invincible argument, which might immediately lead the mind into the pure principles of theism, and make it overleap, at one bound, the vast interval which is interposed between the human and divine nature. But though I allow, that the order and frame of the universe, when accurately examined, affords such an argument; yet I can never think, that this consideration could have an influence on mankind, when they formed their first rude notions of religion. (NHR 1.5)

It is important to note just what Hume is arguing for in this passage. He is admitting that the design evident in the world could lead one to the sophisticated notion of a divine being, but he does not believe that earliest humans would have thought this way. So, despite the early polytheism and belief in inferior gods that one associates with tribal religion, Hume acknowledges that there are also 'the *pure* principles of theism' which give rise to the belief in a purely spiritual Deity, and that it is possible to arrive at this conclusion by 'overleaping, at one bound' the sophisticated inferior gods by recognizing the philosophical force of the design argument.

Hume makes the same point later in the first chapter when he argues that it seems implausible that having once arrived at the pure principles of theism, 'they could never possibly leave that belief, in order to embrace polytheism' (NHR 1.7). Thus, to Hume, it seems that polytheism must have come *first*, otherwise, it seems unlikely that it ever would have become a viable system of belief. In making this point, however, Hume affirms again the origin of monotheism on the basis of the evidence of design in the world, despite the existence of erroneous polytheistic beliefs. Since these affirmations support the main themes of the book, it is inappropriate to read them as ironic.

In the fourth chapter, Hume observes that there is nearly universal con-
sent among people in the affirmation of an 'invisible, intelligent power'.
However, the dispute is whether this being is supreme or subordinate, one
or several, plus other questions as to the attributes of this 'power'. He notes
that his European ancestors believed 'as we do at present' that there is 'one
supreme God, the author of nature' possessed of great power (NHR 4.1).
However, they also believed in 'other invisible powers', like fairies, goblins,
elves and the like. Hume argues that someone who believed in these beings,
but denied the existence of God, would justly be called an atheist. Thus,
a genuine theist is one who does not believe in one of these powers. To
quote Hume, 'The difference, on one hand, between such a person and a
genuine theist is infinitely greater than that, on the other, between him and
one that absolutely excludes all invisible intelligent power' (NHR 4.1).
Hume clarifies this point in the next paragraph. Polytheists and those who
believe in fairies and goblins are really just superstitious atheists, since they
'acknowledge no being, that corresponds to our idea of a deity. No first
principle of mind or thought: No supreme government and administration:
No divine contrivance or intention in the fabric of the world' (NHR 4.2).

Summarizing then, one may observe that Hume has indicated that there
are two accounts of religions' origins. What he terms *genuine theism* corresponds to the belief in a single high god. Polytheism, on the other hand,
invents numerous minor spiritual beings, often possessed of attributes
that are similar to human traits. Hume criticizes this religious tradition as
nothing more than superstitious atheism, and distinguishes it from the
belief that 'we [hold] at present' in the supreme God who is the author
of nature. The important question, of course, is how sincere Hume is in
endorsing what he calls genuine theism.

In answer to this question, the following points are relevant. There are no
internal inconsistencies or outrageous statements that undercut the straightforward meaning of these texts. There are no known errors asserted or any
other explicit clues that suggest irony is at play. The interpretation that
Hume considers himself a theist does not work against the basic theses of
the *Natural History* to date (the priority of polytheism, the abuses of popular
religion). What catches the attention of most readers of Hume, however,
are the interpretational issues that lie in the future, namely, how to reconcile these statements in praise of the design argument with his criticisms of
it in the *Dialogues* and his other sweeping criticisms of religion in the first
Enquiry. These questions, however, do remain in the future, and the answers
to these questions will present themselves as I further investigate Hume's
reflections on the nature of the god and religion.

Hume distinguishes, in chapter 2, between the methods of investigation in the two religious perspectives. Compare these passages:

> Were men led into the apprehension of invisible, intelligent power by a contemplation of the works of nature, they could never possibly entertain any conception but of one single being, who bestowed existence and order on this vast machine, and adjusted all its parts, according to one regular plan or connected system. All things in the universe are evidently of a piece. Every thing is adjusted to every thing. One design prevails throughout the whole. And this uniformity leads the mind to acknowledge one author. (NHR 2.2)

> On the other hand, if, leaving the works of nature, we trace the footsteps of invisible power in the various and contrary events of human life, we are necessarily led into polytheism and to the acknowledgment of several limited and imperfect deities. (NHR 2.3)

The key difference between the two approaches is that the enterprise which leads to the discovery of the one author of all nature begins by considering 'the works of nature', whereas the investigation which leads to a belief in 'several limited and imperfect deities' begins by an examination of the 'various and contrary events of human life', or, as Hume calls it, 'a particular providence'. The attempt to find meaning and purpose behind the events of life will invariably result in polytheism and the attendant superstitions that come from believing in and appeasing a moon god, a sun god, a fertility god and the like. Genuine theism, on the other hand, arises from and is characterized by a philosophical contemplation of the whole of nature, and the adherence to general providence.

A full discussion of the distinction between particular and general providence is one that is best postponed until Chapter 5 in the context of Hume's characterization of the nature of the deity. At this point, however, it is appropriate to note that genuine theism, for Hume, is more philosophical and sophisticated in its understanding of the providential role of God. To be more specific, Hume holds that the deity exercises providential care in an indirect way, through principles that were built into the universe at the time of creation. He opposes a god who resorts to answering prayers or performing miracles or sending punishing calamities. These sorts of beliefs appeal to the vulgar religionists, who prefer to see the hand of God behind every event, and so develop unsophisticated superstitions regarding natural occurrences.

The third chapter yields yet another characteristic distinction between the two religious perspectives. There is among human beings, Hume tells us, a 'universal tendency . . . to conceive all beings like themselves, and to transfer to every object, those qualities, with which they are familiarly acquainted, and of which they are intimately conscious' (NHR 3.2). In other words, we have a propensity to analyze things in terms of ourselves. We reify nature. We attribute feelings, volition, thought and other human characteristics to those things that we observe and imagine. The situation is not different when we reflect on the divine, as Hume notes:

> The absurdity is not less, while we cast our eyes upwards and transferring, as is too usual, human passions and infirmities to the deity, represent him as jealous and revengeful, capricious and partial, and, in short, a wicked and foolish man, in every respect but his superior power and authority. (NHR 3.2)

Thus, the propensity for transferring human characteristics to nonhuman entities leads inevitably to superstition. Hume writes that we 'find human faces in the moon, armies in the clouds; and by a natural propensity, if not corrected by experience and reflection, ascribe malice or goodwill to every thing, that hurts or pleases us' (NHR 3.2). The remedy is proper education, as may be observed in this passage on superstitious people, whose lives are purportedly ruled by accidents and fate.

> Ignorant of astronomy and the anatomy of plants and animals, and too little curious to observe the admirable adjustment of final causes; they remain still unacquainted with a first and supreme creator, and with that infinitely perfect spirit, who alone, by his almighty will, bestowed order on the whole frame of nature (NHR 3.3).

The truly reflective individuals, who marry their natural curiosity with a well-grounded education in the sciences, will come to the realization of a divine spirit who created everything. The simple-minded, on the other hand, will construct numerous minor deities to appease their superstitions and, out of their ignorance, will neglect the greater religious truth of the one true god. The superstitious have another natural propensity, this one to melancholy and despair. Natural fear, Hume argues, leads to polytheism and away from genuine theism. 'The mind, sunk into diffidence, terror and melancholy, has recourse to every method of appeasing those secret intelligent powers, on whom our fortune is supposed entirely to depend' (NHR 3.4).

This theme resurfaces in chapter 5, where Hume continues his investigation into the origins of polytheism and superstition in the propensities of human nature, which must be distinguished from the truths of genuine theism.

> Whoever learns by argument, the existence of invisible intelligent power, must reason from the admirable contrivance of natural objects, and must suppose the world to be the workmanship of that divine being, the original cause of all things. But the vulgar polytheist, so far from admitting that idea, deifies every part of the universe, and conceives all the conspicuous productions of nature, to be themselves so many real divinities. (NHR 5.2)

In addition to the note that proper education and argumentation lead one to the conclusion of a divine creator, two secondary points bear mention.

First, the evidence suggests that Hume's predominant concern was the problem of religious superstition. Although he frequently contrasts the true religion and genuine theism with its vulgar counterparts, he offers sustained analysis only of the superstitious religions. The passage cited above serves as an example of the fact that Hume tends only to mention briefly the correct theistic point of view (from his point of view), while focusing the crux of his attention on the errors and difficulties. This imbalance is, no doubt, in part responsible for the tendency to neglect or overlook Hume's religious affirmations, which appear throughout the *Natural History*, in favor of his criticisms. However, such a neglect obscures his true positions on God and religion. That Hume's treatment is more detailed in critique of superstition and false religion does not, however, justify neglect of his affirmations regarding genuine theism.

Secondly, it is not necessary to take Hume's affirmations of genuine theism as insincere or ironic concessions to society's conventions in order to make sense of his condemnations of the various problems associated with false religion. Put another way, Hume's sharp criticisms of religious practices ancient and contemporary still have bite, whether one understands his affirmation passages as genuine or not. This recognition neutralizes the need that many Hume scholars feel to write off the affirmation passages as insincere.

The sixth chapter contains some important passages regarding the true religion – vulgar religion distinction. Hume ruminates that 'the doctrine of one supreme deity, the author of nature', though ancient in time and spread over 'great and populous nations' and 'all ranks and conditions of men', does not owe its success to 'the prevalent force of those invincible reasons, on which it is undoubtedly founded' (NHR 6.1). In eloquent terms,

Hume asks if an ordinary person – even one of his contemporary Europe-
ans – were to justify his belief in an omnipotent creator, the answer given
would likely be superstitious, despite the fact that sophisticated philosophical evidences are in the offing.

> Even at this day, and in EUROPE, ask any of the vulgar, why he believes in
> an omnipotent creator of the world; he will never mention the beauty of
> final causes, of which he is wholly ignorant: He will not hold out his hand,
> and bid you contemplate the suppleness and variety of joints in his fingers,
> their bending all one way, the counterpoise which they receive from the
> thumb, the softness and fleshy parts of the inside of his hand, with all the
> other circumstances, which render that member fit for the use, to which it
> was destined. To these he has been long accustomed; and he beholds them
> with listlessness and unconcern. He will tell you of the sudden and unex-
> pected death of such a one: The fall and bruise of such another: The
> excessive drought of this season: The cold and rains of another. These he
> ascribes to the immediate operation of providence: And such events, as,
> with good reasoners, are the chief difficulties in admitting a supreme intel-
> ligence, are with him the sole arguments for it. (NHR 6.1)

Rather than appealing to a particular providence, a doctrine that true
religionists recognize as problematic, the genuine theist understands that
'the chief argument for theism' is found in the 'beautiful connexion and
rigid observance of established rules'. The true path has been described by
Francis Bacon, whom Hume cites:

> A *little philosophy*, says lord BACON, *makes men atheists: A great deal reconciles
> them to religion.* For men, being taught, by superstitious prejudices, to lay
> the stress on a wrong place; when that fails them, and they discover, by a
> little reflection, that the course of nature is regular and uniform, their
> whole faith totters, and falls to ruin. But being taught, by more reflection,
> that this very regularity and uniformity is the strongest proof of design
> and of a supreme intelligence, they return to that belief, which they had
> deserted; and they are now able to establish it on a firmer and more
> durable foundation. (NHR 6.2)

These paragraphs reiterate some of the themes from the earlier chapters,
with one new element. The doctrine of one supreme deity, although it
ought to be asserted on the basis of 'final causes' and the evidence of design,
can also result from the superstitious belief in particular providence. It is
possible that some beliefs may arise out of popular theism which coincide
with the tenants of true religion. The best path to true religion is through

philosophy, as Bacon asserted. This assertion undergirds Hume's position that true religion is a species of true philosophy, and that proper education leads to genuine theism.

However, there is an interesting overlap between some of the tenets of genuine theism and those of vulgar theism which muddles this clean distinction.

Convulsions in nature, disorder, prodigies, miracles, though the opposite of the plan of a wise superintendent, impress mankind with the strongest sentiments of religion; the causes of events seeming then the most unknown and unaccountable. Madness, fury, rage, and an inflamed imagination, though they sink men nearest to the level of beasts, are, for a like reason, often supposed to be the only dispositions, in which we can have any immediate communication with the Deity. We may conclude, therefore, upon the whole, that, since the vulgar, in nations, which have embraced the doctrine of theism, still build it upon irrational and superstitious principles, they are never led into that opinion by any process of argument, but by a certain train of thinking, more suitable to their genius and capacity. (NHR 6.3–4)

A problem for Hume's two different stories regarding the origin of religion is that some of the vulgar do believe in one god, which, according to his analysis, is only characteristic of genuine theism. The solution that Hume offers is to qualify his analysis to allow for a *coincidence* of belief, even though they spring from different sources. It is possible for the vulgar theist to come to a true proposition about the existence of one god, but it is a happenstance and not based on discursive reasoning. The greater the fears and superstitions of a particular people, the more they are likely to raise one of their deities to increasing higher levels, thus stumbling by chance onto philosophical truths about the nature of the divine being.

Thus they proceed [with their adulations]; till at last they arrive at infinity itself, beyond which there is no farther progress: And it is well, if, in striving to get farther, and to represent a magnificent simplicity, they run not into inexplicable mystery, and destroy the intelligent nature of their deity, on which alone any rational worship or adoration can be founded. While they confine themselves to the notion of a perfect being, the creator of the world, they coincide, by chance, with the principles of reason and true philosophy; though they are guided to that notion, not by reason, of which they are in a great measure incapable, but by the adulation and fears of the most vulgar superstition. (NHR 6.5)

This critical passage makes it clear that Hume finds the belief in one supreme god that exists in some vulgar religions a matter of coincidence. True religion arises out of true philosophy, and while the superstitious may believe in one god, they are incapable of doing true philosophy. Thus, they are excluded from following true religion. That they hold some true religious propositions does not alter this fundamental state of affairs.

To summarize the analysis that I have been offering of the *Natural History* thus far, I find two stories of the origin of religious belief and practice. The predominant story is of false religion, which is built on the superstitions that result from natural human propensities, such as fear and the tendency to humanize nonhuman entities. The characteristic consequence of these propensities is the invention of numerous spirits and minor deities, to whom people must offer all manner of religious ceremony and worship in the hopes of securing the gods' favor. The common folk, then, believe in a particular providence, place great confidence in their priests and religious authorities, and fail to escape this unfortunate worldview because of their lack of suitable education and exposure to true philosophy.

The second story is not developed in as much detail as the first story, and pointedly almost never exemplified in Hume's analysis. It is, however, the story of true religion, which discovers the one true and surpassing God, who created all and governs the universe according to his eternal laws, written out of his supreme power and wisdom. These truths are only accessible through true philosophy, as seen in the argument for design and the necessity for a first cause. Over and over in these initial chapters, Hume affirms the second story in contradistinction to the errors and misjudgments of the first story. In chapter 7, Hume does offer the story of the Getes, who are 'genuine theists' that affirmed their deity to be 'the only true god'. Nevertheless, their true belief did not prevent them from superstitious ritual, in this case, human sacrifice. This example reveals Hume's frustration with the fact that even true religion is prone to abuses and abominations.

If one accepts this two story interpretation, then it is possible to interpret the last paragraph of chapter 6 in a mostly straightforward way, despite the fact that, at first glance, it appears to be nothing more than an example of Hume's sarcastic wit and savage irony.

> Were there a religion (and we may suspect Mahometanism [Islam] of this inconsistence) which sometimes painted the Deity in the most sublime colours, as the creator of heaven and earth; sometimes degraded him nearly to the level with human creatures in his powers and faculties; while at the same time it ascribed to him suitable infirmities, passions and

partialities, of the moral kind: That religion, after it was extinct, would also be cited as an instance of those contradictions, which arise from the gross, vulgar, natural conceptions of mankind, opposed to their continual propensity towards flattery and exaggeration. Nothing indeed would prove more strongly the divine origin of any religion, than to find (and happily this is the case with Christianity) that it is free from a contradiction, so incident to human nature. (NHR 6.12)

It is not necessary to read the last sentence of this paragraph as a ringing endorsement of Christianity in order to maintain the interpretation that I have been defending, nor to write the entire paragraph off as simply an extended irony. This sentence displays at least one of the telltale signs of irony, namely, that it conflicts with established facts.

The Bible does often present God in the 'contradictory' fashion which Hume attributes to Islam. There is frequent use of anthropomorphic language in that there is mention of God's eyes, his arm, even his back. In addition, God is said to have emotions (anger, love and jealousy, among others), and even, at times, to change his mind, while at the same time possessing the transcendental attributes which Hume links to genuine theism. And most importantly, the central Christian doctrine of the incarnation of Jesus is a blatant mixing of the 'sublime colours' of the Deity with human degradation. Certainly, Hume was aware of this inconsistency between his comments about Christianity and the true state of affairs. Thus, it is important to see Hume poking some fun at those serious divines who understood their religion to be so superior to the superstitious and unsophisticated rants of the primitive polytheists.

Natural History of Religion: Flux and Reflux

The second half of the Natural History begins with the eighth chapter, where Hume develops the major theme of the 'flux and reflux' between monotheism and polytheism. People, Hume argues, 'have a natural tendency to rise from idolatry to theism, and to sink again from theism into idolatry.' (NHR 8.1). There is, according to Hume, a cycle that operates in the history of religion, a fluctuation between theism and polytheism. This oscillation between monotheism and polytheism would seem to present some problems for the two story interpretation that I have been defending. If there are two distinct accounts of the origin of religious traditions, then it would seem impossible that there would be a cycle, since the cycle implies a single, oscillating account. Given the introduction of the cycle notion, one may wonder at the veracity of the two story interpretation.

One rejoinder is to recall that Hume has already qualified the two story account by allowing for coincidental beliefs. It does happen that the superstitious believers will stumble on the doctrine of monotheism, but this is mere happenstance and not true philosophy. Is it possible that the cycles of polytheism and monotheism are the result of accidental insights on the part of the superstitious? The answer, it seems, is yes and no. The coincidental beliefs do occur, but these occurrences are not sufficient to explain the phenomena of the cycle. It is important to pay close attention to Hume's analysis of the cycle in the beginning of chapter 8.

> The vulgar, that is, all mankind, a few excepted, being ignorant and uninstructed, never elevate their contemplation to the heavens, or penetrate by their disquisitions into the secret structure of vegetable or animal bodies; so far as to discover a supreme mind or original providence, which bestowed order on every part of nature. . . . The unknown causes are still appealed to on every emergence; and in this general appearance or confused image, are the perpetual objects of human hopes and fears, wishes and apprehensions. By degrees, the active imagination of men, uneasy in this abstract conceptions of objects, about which it is incessantly employed, begins to render them more particular, and to clothe them in shapes more suitable to its natural comprehension. It represents them to be sensible, intelligent being, like mankind; actuated by love and hatred, and flexible by gifts and entreaties, by prayers and sacrifices. Hence the origin of religion: And hence the origin of idolatry or polytheism. (NHR 8.1)

This important passage begins by revealing one of the main reasons why Hume's analysis is imbalanced, with the far greater treatment devoted to false, vulgar religion. It is because the vulgar comprise all of mankind, only 'a few excepted'. The relative scarcity of adherents of the true religion is a theme that will resurface in the *Dialogues*, but it is a significant part of Hume's analysis here in the *Natural History*. Since only a small number escape the idolatry of the superstitious, Hume turns his full attention to the vulgar, and he will have almost nothing to say regarding true religion or genuine theism until the last chapter. The vulgar, Hume theorizes, are never able to elevate their contemplations and disquisitions to a true conception of a 'supreme mind or original providence'. They never discover the religious insights of true philosophy, because they are consumed with their own happiness or misery, and they focus their attention on the 'unknown causes of their particular circumstances'. They never escape the trap of particular providence, and so gradually, they bring their 'abstract conception[s]' down to their more familiar world. These abstract conceptions eventually become particular and human, and, thus, the vulgar invent their gods in their own image.

There is a kind of vulgar theism, even a kind of vulgar monotheism, but it is never more than incidentally related to the genuine theism of the few followers of true religion. Inevitably, this vulgar theism is brought down to the level of polytheism and idolatry, until such time as the vulgar begin to elevate their gods again in a never-to-be-successful attempt to ascend to a true conception of the one god. Thus, the cycle is always a part of false religion. The monotheistic period of the cycle is still false religion. It resembles genuine theism only coincidentally, since its beginning is in vulgar theism. It can never be true theism, since that comes from a different story altogether.[11]

In the ensuing chapters, Hume continues to develop his thesis of the cycle between (false) monotheism and polytheism, and, as a result, his criticism of religious ceremonies and practices (all of which are species of superstition) becomes more pointed. There is no mention of genuine theism after chapter 8, until the concluding chapter of the book. In chapter 9, Hume compares the advantages and disadvantages of both parts of the cycle. Under polytheism, there is tolerance, which Hume, true Enlightenment son that he is, recognizes as a positive state of affairs. However, the cost of the toleration is that all practices can be justified, thus undercutting any contribution that religious belief can make to ethics. On the other hand, vulgar theism can help to establish a moral framework, but only by practicing intolerance towards other systems of belief. More examples of this dilemma are addressed in the following chapters, and it is not necessary to rehearse all of the aspects of this dilemma, given that all religious developments within the cycle are to be distinguished from genuine theism. Hume did not frequently make this distinction explicitly, but it is apparent in a passage in chapter 13, where Hume characterizes both ends of the cycle as 'popular religion' and described, in turn, the errors of both aspects (NHR 13.6).

It is only in the 15th and final chapter that Hume returns to the language and the themes that characterize the two stories of genuine theism and vulgar religion. He proclaims again the evidence of design that is apparent in all the universe.

A purpose, an intention, a design is evident in every thing; and when our comprehension is so far enlarged as to contemplate the first rise of this visible system, we must adopt, with the strongest convictions, the idea of some intelligent cause or author. The uniform maxims, too, which prevail throughout the whole frame of nature of the universe, naturally, if not necessarily, lead us to conceive this intelligence as single and undivided, where the prejudices of education oppose not so reasonable a theory. Even the contrarieties of nature, by discovering themselves every where, become proofs of some consistent plan, and establish one single purpose or intention, however inexplicable and incomprehensible. (NHR 15.1)

The confident affirmations at the commencement of the passage devolve, however, into states of mind which are 'inexplicable and incomprehensible', attitudes which also characterize the well-known ending of the book. Hume famously concludes that the whole of religion is 'a riddle, an enigma, an inexplicable mystery. Doubt, uncertainly, suspense of judgment appear the only result of our most accurate scrutiny, concerning this subject'. Hume's solution to this bewildering state of affairs that attends religion is to flee to the 'calm, though obscure, regions of philosophy' (NHR 15.13).

What is it exactly that confounds Hume, and does this irreducible riddle mean that he is rejecting his earlier affirmations regarding genuine theism and true religion?

Hume perceives a contradictory state of affairs in the world. There is genuine theism, which is derived from observations of the handiwork of the creator, and there are rational individuals who are privileged to be able to reflect on these wonderful truths. However, there are also the false, popular religions, which besmirch the deity by imagining him to be comparable to human beings. These false conceptions are what characterize most of religious practice and belief. What Hume finds unfortunate, even tragic, in these circumstances is that there is no good reason for the persistence of these popular religions, when true religion can be discovered. It is the actuality of both religious traditions, present simultaneously in the world, plus the fact that false religion is overwhelmingly dominant in 'most nations and most ages', that perplexes and dismays Hume. It is the inability of the true notions of religion (as Hume sees it) to do away with the false and popular beliefs that Hume finds a riddle and an enigma.

His advice to return to philosophy, then, is not a repudiation of his earlier affirmations of genuine theism. In fact, it is the opposite. True religion is a species of true philosophy, and it is by proper philosophizing that one discovers true religion. Returning then to philosophy is the first step on the pathway to the true religion and genuine theism that Hume affirms repeatedly throughout this work. A careful reading of the *Natural History of Religion* reveals much of Hume's authentic beliefs regarding God. There is a god, a transcendent being, who is the first cause and creator of the world, a being who ought not be demeaned by thoughtless comparisons to human beings. Evidence for the existence of the deity is clear from the marks of design and purpose which one can observe throughout the world. Scholars who are only familiar with Hume through the *Dialogues* may find this conclusion difficult to accept, given the commonly accepted notion that it is one long critique of the argument from design. The next task that awaits is to show that the *Dialogues* support, and do not contradict, the interpretation of Hume's thoughts on God and religion that emerge from the *Natural History*.

Dialogues concerning Natural Religion: Who Speaks for Hume?

The *Dialogues concerning Natural Religion* also have an eventful publication history. Originally written in the early 1750s, Hume circulated a perhaps incomplete version of the *Dialogues* to some friends to solicit their advice regarding potential publication and even for their assistance with some of the dialogue.[12] These confidants persuaded Hume not to publish, presumably on the grounds that the work would be too controversial. There is evidence to suggest that Hume worked on the *Dialogues* for several years and then put them away for some 15 years, until the last year of his life, when he resumed editing and polishing them. They were much on his mind during the final summer of his life, and he frequently corresponded with Adam Smith in an effort to have Smith agree to publish them posthumously for him. This task Smith declined, but Hume's nephew saw to it that they were published about three years after Hume's death. They are, undoubtedly, a philosophical masterpiece, comparable to the superb dialogues of Plato and Cicero, and one of the best books on the philosophy of religion ever written.

A substantial part of the *Dialogues*' enduring value is the difficulty that one finds in interpreting them. They are more successful than most of Plato's dialogues in the task of forcing the reader to see the strengths and weaknesses of the various arguments from both an advocate's and an adversary's point of view. The thoughtful reader, whether theist or atheist, is unable to read the whole book without finding his or her positions challenged and presuppositions tested.

The number of different interpretations of the *Dialogues* is staggering, and I will not attempt to catalogue all of them. Nor I will attempt to interpret the whole of the work. In order to defend my overall thesis that Hume affirmed the existence of God, it is not necessary to follow all of its twists and turns. My main interpretive tasks are to discuss the problem of who speaks for Hume, to explore the affirmation statements of all the interlocutors, to distinguish the two arguments from design that are presented, and to show how Part 12 coheres with the rest of the book. The final goal will be to show how the true religion that Hume described in the *Natural History* is also advocated in the *Dialogues*.

One of the perennial questions regarding the *Dialogues* is ascertaining which of the interlocutors speaks for Hume. Historically, the most popular choice is the skeptical Philo, which is the position of Kemp Smith, Flew, Gaskin, Mossner, Penelhum, Pike, Schmidt and others.[13] Prior to Kemp Smith, some Hume scholars (like Andre Leroy and A. E. Taylor) identified Cleanthes as Hume's spokesman.[14] Hume himself lends credence to this point of view in a letter which enlists the help of Gilbert Elliot with the composition of the *Dialogues*. Hume writes, 'You wou'd perceive by the Sample I have given you, that I make Cleanthes the Hero of the Dialogue' (L 72; 1.153). However, the idea that Cleanthes is Hume's hero is nullified by the comment that he would like Eliot's help with Cleanthes' arguments and that he feels more comfortable articulating Philo's speeches. One prominent Hume scholar, Charles Hendel, even identified Hume with Pamphilus and his occasional observations about the conversations.[15]

Other interpreters have argued that all the interlocutors speak for Hume at one point or another. This position is endorsed by Yandell,[16] and it is true that each of the major interlocutors offers positions that Hume endorses in other places. For instance, Demea articulates a version of the *bundle theory* of personal identity (DNR 4.2) that Hume presents in T 1.4.6. Cleanthes' criticism of the idea of necessary existence (DNR 9.5–6) resonates with Hume's critiques of necessary connections in the *Treatise*, while Philo's doubting posture is clearly consistent with Hume's own mitigated skepticism. A similar perspective is offered by Anders Jeffner in *Butler and Hume on Religion*.

There is another camp of scholars in this debate that calls into question the assumption that it is possible or even important to determine who speaks for Hume. Miguel Badia Cabrera asserts that, at best, the search for Hume's 'authentic voice' is a secondary affair, and the preoccupation with this question is, on the whole, an 'unprofitable philosophical exercise'.[17] William Lad Sessions likewise questions the underlying premise 'that the *Dialogues* actually were intended by Hume to express his own views via some character speaking directly or ironically'.[18]

My position is consistent with this perspective, in that I hold that the best way to interpret this book is to view the dialogues themselves – as opposed to an individual interlocutor – as representative of what Hume intends to convey. In other words, Hume's point of view cannot be solely reduced to one character, rather he intends the reader to reflect on the weaknesses and strengths of each interlocutor, and thus to distill the truths that emerge from the froth of the entire debate. This interpretation, therefore, puts a great deal of emphasis on the last part, as Cleanthes, Philo and even Pamphilus sum up the salient truths that emerge from the discussions, and so it will be necessary to show that Part 12 is consonant with the whole of the dialogues.

Regardless of whether the dialogues as a whole speak for Hume or a specific interlocutor does, it requires little thought to ascertain that Philo is the critical individual for my thesis that Hume believes that there is a god and that this conclusion is evident in the *Dialogues*. Even if one grants the position that the dialogues speak for Hume, Philo's proclaimed skepticism makes him the individual inherently most resistant to theistic belief. If it is shown that Philo's skepticism is overcome such that he sincerely affirms the existence of God, then the conclusion naturally seems to follow that Hume himself intends this conclusion. Jeffner argued that if two of the interlocutors agreed with each other, the implication then is that they speak for Hume. Taking Jeffner's principle that two concurring interlocutors represent Hume a bit further, if all *three* interlocutors are united in a conclusion, the natural inference is that Hume also shares this belief.

Dialogues concerning Natural Religion: Affirmation Texts & Two Arguments from Design

The conversations begin with Pamphilus' observation that what is obvious in natural religion is 'the *being* of a God, which the most ignorant ages have acknowledged, for which the most refined geniuses have ambitiously striven to produce new proofs and arguments' (DNR Intro.5). What is obscure and uncertain, however, is the '*nature* of that Divine Being; his attributes, his decrees, his plan of providence. These have been always subjected to the disputations of men: Concerning these, human reason has not reached any certain determinations' (DNR Intro.5).

This initial contention of the clear existence of the deity is echoed by each of the three main interlocutors on several occasions, although amidst this chorus of agreement, there are also some immediate differences. Philo

quickly asserts the necessity of skepticism, being cognizant of the weaknesses of human reason. Demea agrees with Philo, since this point coincides
with his fideist tendencies. Cleanthes, however, takes issue and wonders at
the extent of Philo's skepticism. 'Whether your scepticism be as absolute
and sincere as you pretend, we shall learn by and by, when the company
breaks up; we shall then see whether you go out at the door or the window'
(DNR 1.5). This slight jab serves, I believe, an important purpose in alerting
the reader that Philo ultimately is not (nor can he be) a Pyrrhonian skeptic.
His mitigated skepticism has bounds, which helps to explain how he can
explore so many skeptical objections to Cleanthes' arguments through the
middle part of the *Dialogues*, and yet still return to a theistic point of view in
the end.

Despite these concessions, Cleanthes still wonders if Philo is not too
skeptical, given that the remarkable advances of Newtonian science seem
to be in concert with the 'religious hypothesis', which is that the existence
of a deity may be asserted on the basis of scientific, empirical evidence.
(DNR 1.16) Cleanthes mentions Bacon's aphorism that a little philosophy
produces atheism, but a great deal leads converts to religion, while Philo
cites Bacon's accusation that atheists commit a double folly, namely, impru-
dent thinking (by denying so obvious a truth) and impiety (presumably in
lying about not believing such a clear proposition). The implication of this
remark is, significantly, that already in the first part, Philo admits to a theistic
point of view. Whether, of course, Philo is being sincere at this juncture
remains to be seen.

Further conversation in Part 1 recalls distinctions observed in the *Natural
History* between true and vulgar religion, which, despite their very different
origins, may still have some coincidental beliefs. Cleanthes is more forgiv-
ing of the abuses of priests and popular religion, since he focuses on the
elements that are shared with true religion (like theistic belief) while Philo
consistently rails against the beliefs of the vulgar, and in so doing, forms a
somewhat unlikely partnership with Demea. Cleanthes and Philo, meanwhile, agree on the existence and nature of the true religion. Demea, as will
be seen, also affirms that there is a true religion, but his beliefs are generally
to be identified with vulgar religion. All three, however, believe in a god,
thus representing the coincidence of vulgar and genuine theism.

The second part commences with Demea's declaration that since the
existence of God is 'so certain and self-evident', the whole of the conversation should be about the nature of God. Alas, the character of that divine
being is 'altogether incomprehensible and unknown to us' (DNR 2.1).
Therefore, the proper perspective is a fideistic one in which the otherness

of God is emphasized, and the likeness of God to human beings is severely minimized.

Demea's declaration of the self-evidency of God in DNR 2.1 is the first of a series of major affirmation statements in Part 2 from each of the main interlocutors. Philo's affirmation statement echoes Demea's in many respects, excepting one significant difference. He agrees that the existence of God is obvious and concurs that God's nature is mysterious. The rub, however, is in Philo's endorsement of the evidence of design – only an undertone at this point – which also runs counter to Demea's preference for a priori argumentation. The result is that Demea is fooled into thinking that Philo is his unqualified ally.

[Philo speaking] But surely, where reasonable men treat these subjects, the question can never be concerning the *being*, but only the *nature* of the Deity. The former truth, as you well observe, is unquestionable and self-evident. Nothing exists without a cause; and the original cause of this universe (whatever it be) we call *God*, and piously ascribe to him every species of perfection. (DNR 2.3)

Cleanthes follows with his affirmation text, which is the much-discussed Machine Analogy. He asserts that the world is 'nothing but one great machine', characterized by an incredible complexity and intricacy, which 'resembles exactly, though it much exceeds, the productions of human contrivance'. The result of this analogy is that 'the Author of nature is somewhat similar to the mind of man, though possessed of much larger faculties' (DNR 2.5).

Thus, each of the characters affirm in strong language the existence of God, but the lines of disagreement are nevertheless drawn. Philo and Demea hold that the divine being is fundamentally unknowable and dissimilar from humans, while Cleanthes argues for analogous intelligence between people and God. On the other hand, Philo and Cleanthes are united in their support for the evidence for design (although the specific arguments that they will employ are different), while Demea maintains that a posteriori argumentation is entirely unsuccessful and inappropriate with regard to the deity.

Some readers will assume that since each interlocutor affirms the existence of God, Hume must intend irony, at the very least, for Philo's concession. However, none of the five clues that would signal irony have appeared. For instance, one might suspect irony if the conversations seem contrived or the debates lacking in substance, or if one of the characters is inconsistent with statements he makes at other places. On the contrary, however, taking the comments at face value reveals the rigor and complexity of the debate, as befitting a multifaceted discussion.

Specifically with regard to Philo, I will show that there is a consistency in his comments throughout the *Dialogues*, which also undercuts the possibility that his comments are to be understood ironically. It is true that Philo is clever and sometimes baits Demea into concluding that they are in agreement to a larger degree than they really are. This circumstance is a mild form of irony, although it is probably just as easily understood as Demea's self-deception, rather than Philo's subterfuge. The broader point, however, is that there is no large scale recourse to irony which requires the reader to understand the true intent of Hume to be much different from the natural meaning of the conversations.

Returning to the debates themselves, it seems that one of the most misunderstood aspects of the *Dialogues* is the relationship of Philo to the argument from design. Philo affirms over and over, throughout the whole course of the work, his esteem for the evidence of design that he observes in the world. This evidence is empirical and scientific, and it leads to the inevitable conclusion that there is a First Cause, a Creator who fashioned the universe. Besides the brief hint regarding the original cause (already cited from DNR 2.3) there are also these passages in which Philo affirms his belief that the evidence of design infers the existence of a deity: DNR 5.2, 6.12, 10.36, 11.11, 12.2–4, 12.6–8, 12.32.

It is true that Philo critiques Cleanthes' arguments, and he even attempts (at times, as in Parts 6 and 7) to explain the evidence for design in ways that are in opposition to a traditional theistic point of view. The reason that Philo seems to sometimes be in favor of the design argument and at other times opposed to it is that there are really *two* design arguments in play, one which Cleanthes presents and which leads to some unfounded conclusions regarding the nature of the deity, and one which Philo asserts and which does not demean the character of God by comparing him to humans. In addition, Philo's skeptical methodology means that he will subject the proffered assertions to the strongest objections that he can discover, confident that the true proposition will survive the examination. It is for these reasons that the middle parts of the *Dialogues* may initially seem to be inconsistent with Part 12, however, in the end, there is no true reversal on Philo's part.

The first design argument is the Machine Analogy presented by Cleanthes and immediately challenged by both Demea and Philo. They are united in claiming that this analogy is demeaning to God. Philo also raises some logical objections, namely, that we only observe a small part of the known universe, so it is illegitimate to generalize about the cause of the whole thing (DNR 2.19–20). In addition, since both the universe and the purported god are unique things, it is unacceptable to generalize about them (DNR 2.24).

Cleanthes' rejoinders – the Articulate Voice and Vegetable Library thought experiments – have been the subject of some interesting debates in the secondary literature. Some, like Nelson Pike, see them as ultimately carrying the day for Cleanthes, but others find them less than persuasive. The first thought experiment supposes that an 'articulate voice' is suddenly heard over all the earth, at the same time, and conveying a cogent message understood by everyone in their own language. The point, Cleanthes argues, is that upon hearing such a voice, one would immediately conclude that there is an intelligent cause behind this state of affairs (DNR 3.2).

The second thought experiment imagines that books could grow naturally, as vegetables do, and that they are written in a natural, innate and universal human language. If such a 'vegetable library' could be grown, which contained an intelligent sense and order, who could doubt that there must be some kind of intelligence behind this production? As bizarre as this scenario sounds, Cleanthes makes the point that the best books we do have (like the *Iliad* or *Aeneid*) – clearly products of superior human minds – are, nevertheless, dwarfed by the superior complexity and intricacy of naturally occurring things like trees and squirrels. 'But if there be any difference, Philo, between this supposed case [the vegetative books] and the real one of the universe, it is all to the advantage of the latter. The anatomy of the animals affords many stronger instances of design than the perusal of *Livy* or *Tacitus*' (DNR 3.6).

Cleanthes asserts in forceful tones that his 'religious argument' is not susceptible to Philo's skepticism. He challenges Philo that his mitigated skepticism compels him to accept those arguments which 'adhere to common sense and the plain instincts of nature; and to assent, wherever any reasons strike him with so full a force that he cannot, without the greatest violence, prevent it' (DNR 3.7). The following excerpts from Cleanthes' stirring challenge conclude his defense of the Machine Analogy. Without a doubt, these words are the highpoint of Cleanthes' participation in the discussions, and mark a very important turning point in the *Dialogues*:

Now the arguments for natural religion are plainly of this kind; and nothing but the most perverse, obstinate metaphysics can reject them. Consider, anatomize the eye: survey its structure and contrivance, and tell me, from your own feeling, if the idea of a contriver does not immediately flow in upon you with a force like that of sensation. The most obvious conclusion, surely, is in favor of design; and it requires time, reflection, and study, to summon up those frivolous thought abstruse objections which can support infidelity. . . . And if the arguments for theism be, as you pretend, contradictory to the principles of logic, its irresistible influence proves clearly that there may be arguments of a like irregular nature. Whatever cavils may be urged; an orderly world, as well as a coherent, articulate speech, will still be received as an incontestable proof of design and intention. (DNR 3.7–8)

The significance of this eloquent speech is evident in the effect that Pamphilus observes in Philo, who is found to be 'a little embarrassed or confounded' (DNR 3.10). Although Pamphilus does not specify the exact reason for Philo's discomfort, it is no stretch to surmise that Cleanthes' words have found their mark, but to what degree is a debated question. Kemp Smith views Cleanthes' arguments in Parts 2 and 3 as ultimately rather weak, but, he thinks that Hume is forced to maintain the illusion that Philo was really confounded by Cleanthes' presentation in order to maintain the dramatic balance between the interlocutors. In the final analysis, however, Kemp Smith contends that 'Philo has the situation very well in hand, and can afford to stand back, while Demea entangles Cleanthes in yet further admissions.'[19]

Other readers of the *Dialogues* view the impact of Cleanthes' speech differently. P. S. Wadia takes issue with Kemp Smith, arguing that Cleanthes does succeed in turning Philo from some of his earlier skeptical musings, with the effect that the discussion focuses on the question of the nature of God, and not his existence, from this point.[20] Nelson Pike sees even greater repercussions from Cleanthes' speech. He places great emphasis on the *irregular* nature of the argument, in which 'the inference does not involve consideration of an empirically established correlation between classes. It is drawn *directly* from the data – it "immediately flows in upon you with a force like that of sensation"'.[21] According to Pike, while Philo could raise logical objections to the Machine Analogy, he cannot raise objections to this 'irregular argument'. Thus, his confounding in Part 3 is a precursor to his affirmations in Part 12, and the roots of Philo's confessions at the end of the *Dialogues* are in the persuasiveness of Cleanthes' irregular argument.[22]

I support Pike's interpretation to a point, but his explication of the reason why Philo capitulates to Cleanthes is inadequate. I think that Pike misunderstands the precise significance of Cleanthes' language regarding the irregular argument, even though he does highlight the specific phrases in question. Cleanthes challenges his listeners that, after they anatomize the eye and survey its structure, they should tell 'from their own feeling, if the idea of a contriver does not immediately flow in upon you with a force like that of sensation', and that it will be necessary 'to assent [to any argument], wherever any reasons strike him with so full a force that he cannot, without the greatest violence, prevent it' (DNR 3.7).

I suggest that Cleanthes is referring to what Hume described in the *Treatise* as an *impression of reflection*. Hume distinguished two kinds of impressions, to wit, those which arise directly from sensation, and also those which are the products of reflection. The latter are also known as passions, and Cleanthes specifically challenges his listeners to see if they do not *feel* the force of the evidence for design, in a way not unlike the way one feels pain or cold.

Hume described the process of receiving an impression of reflection as beginning with an ordinary impression of sensation, which produces a feeling of pleasure or pain that is copied to the mind. In turn, then, these feelings produce feelings of aversion or desire, which eventually become ideas, which can produce more impressions of reflection (T 1.1.2.1). It seems that something similar happens with the evidence for design. Viewing the complexity of the eye results in an impression which excites feelings of wonder or perhaps awe. These feelings strike us with a force like sensation, and it is as if we have witnessed first-hand the fashioning of the human eye by the hand of God. It must be admitted that having an impression of God is not typically how one understands Hume's epistemology, but one must remember that this argument is characterized as 'irregular'. It may not be typical empiricist reasoning, but Hume has Cleanthes make an interesting case for it, and that in a way that conforms with his own teachings.

Further support for cognizing God as a result of impressions of reflection is found in EHU 2.6. 'The idea of God, as meaning *an infinitely intelligent, wise and good Being*, arises from reflecting on the operations of our own mind, and augmenting, without limit, those qualities of goodness and wisdom.' Although in this text Hume does not distinguish between a humanly constructed deity, or the true god, it seems as though the notion of God is discovered through reflection on the evidence of design.[23]

Philo, confounded and convinced (at least partially) by Cleanthes' irregular argument, does not lose his wits. He regroups by capitulating to the design argument, but one of a different stripe. Philo's version can be traced from the beginning of Part 5:

Like effects prove like causes. This is the experimental argument; and this, you say too, is the sole theological argument. Now it is certain, that the

liker the effects are, which are seen, and the liker the causes, which are
inferred, the stronger is the argument. Every departure on either side
diminishes the probability, and renders the experiment less conclusive.
You cannot doubt of this principle: Neither ought you to reject its consequences. All the new discoveries in astronomy, which prove the immense
grandeur and magnificence of the works of nature are so many additional
arguments for a Deity, according to the true system of theism: But,
according to your hypothesis of experimental theism, they become so
many objections, by removing the effect still farther from all resemblance
to the effects of human art and contrivance. (DNR 5.1–2)

In holding out for a second argument from design, Philo sides with Demea,
because he wants to avoid the dark implication of Cleanthes' experimental
theism, namely, that if the characteristics of the deity are displayed in
the universe, then one cannot escape the conclusion that God is morally
culpable for all the evil in the world.

In order to escape these ruinous implications, Philo prefers a design
argument which does *not* include an analogy between the Creator and the
created. Now, it must be admitted that Philo never traces out such an argument to the detail that Cleanthes does. What Philo does assert over and
over is that the evidence from design makes for a strong inference to a
divine creator. The 'immense grandeur and magnificence' of the world
prompts 'so many additional arguments' for the deity, which was exactly the
point that was reiterated about genuine theism at many places in the *Natural
History*. So, while Philo may not ever make his argument explicit in all of its
premises and conclusions, there can be no doubt that he has such an argument in mind.

It would not be a difficult task to construct such an argument for Philo.
Kemp Smith observes that the design argument of Cleanthes was a popular
version of the teleological argument in Hume's day, but it is far from the
only kind of design argument. 'This argument, it cannot be too emphati-
cally insisted, is not a teleological argument of the Aristotelian type. It is an
essentially anthropomorphic type of argument, resting upon an alleged
analogy between natural existences and the artificial products of man's
handicraft.'[24] Aquinas' Fifth Way, for example, does not require an analogy.
The presence of order suggests purpose, and purpose demands an agent,
who stands behind the whole process.

Pike holds that Philo ultimately accepts Cleanthes' irregular argumentation and incorporates it into his own way of thinking.[25] Philo's version of the
design argument contains the same kind of immediacy that characterizes

the impression of reflection element of the irregular argument, and so it is plausible to recognize a debt to Cleanthes on this point. Rejecting any analogical premise, Philo's teleological stance moves from observation of design in the world to the immediate inference of a designer, in much the same way that an impression of reflection is grasped. If this interpretation is correct, it would help to distinguish Hume's reliance on natural religion from the English deists' approach. Hume relies on natural religion only to arrive at the conclusion of a creator god, which is thus based on an impression and not demonstration, while the English deists (like Tindal) believe that in nature the whole gospel is published and discoverable.

In Part 6, while sporting with Cleanthes over the fact that his experimental theism could just as easily produce an analogy between the world and an animal, thus making God a kind of soul, Philo nevertheless affirms his attraction to a system of cosmology that 'ascribes an eternal, inherent principle of order to the world' (DNR 6.12). Further on, he elaborates:

> How could things have been as they are, were there not an original inherent principle of order somewhere, in thought or in matter? And it is very indifferent to which of these we give the preference. Chance has no place, on any hypothesis, sceptical or religious. (DNR 6.12)

Although Philo is still keeping some of his cosmological options open to him in order to refute Cleanthes' particular version of the design argument, he still maintains his belief in the presence of order and purpose in the universe.

In Part 10, the most formidable objection to Cleanthes' Machine Analogy is raised, which is the problem of evil. Philo and Demea unite against Cleanthes, although once again the closeness of their alliance is deceiving. Demea upholds the thesis that there is evil and misery in the world, believing that this state of affairs supports his fideistic point of view, since a person burdened with misery will tend to reach out in faith to the God who is over all. Philo agrees with the premise that evil exists, but not Demea's conclusion. Philo raises the problem of suffering, because it is the best argument against Cleanthes' analogically based experimental theism. At the end of the section, Philo proclaims his victory.

> Here, Cleanthes, I find myself at ease in my argument. Here I triumph. Formerly, when we argued concerning the natural attributes of intelligence and design, I needed all my sceptical and metaphysical subtilty to elude your grasp. . . . It is your turn now to tug the laboring oar, and to

support your philosophical subtilties against the dictates of plain reason and experience. (DNR 10.36)

Philo concedes that he required recourse to all of his skeptical arguments in order to refute the Machine Analogy, a task that was made more difficult because he ultimately holds that the 'beauty and fitness of final causes strikes us with such irresistible force that all objections appear (what I believe they really are) mere cavils and sophisms.' He admits that he proposed theories and objections which he really did not believe, simply because they weakened the effectiveness of Cleanthes' analogy. But now that he has finally triumphed by showing that the Machine Analogy is unequipped to give a satisfactory reply to the problem of evil, he can renounce all his skeptical tricks in order to embrace his own design argument, an argument that immediately concludes to a designer without recourse to analogy. As for Cleanthes' response, it is sufficient simply to say that he weakly admits in Part 11 that the best rejoinder the Machine Analogy can offer is that the deity is 'finitely perfect', an oxymoron that is hopelessly unorthodox and utterly unsatisfying to the traditional theist.

One important topic that must be addressed prior to turning attention to the discussion of true religion in the final part is the degree of intellectual distance that separates Cleanthes and Philo leading up the Part 12. In that part, they appear to agree on many points of natural theology, at least more than they had previously. This sudden harmony is one of the reasons that it appears that Philo has reversed himself and, thus, many readers are led to believe that he is being insincere in his affirmations. Sessions, however, contends that, despite their spirited debates, the actual distance between them in terms of the main questions of natural religion is slight. 'Philo's real disagreement with Cleanthes, as we shall see in Part 12, is not over the existence or even the nature of the deity, but rather over the *degree of likeness* between human and divine attributes.'[26] If Sessions is right (and I believe that his argument is clearly borne out by the text), the nearness of Philo and Cleanthes prior to Part 12 will facilitate the interpretation of Part 12 as a natural culmination of the previous eleven parts, and not as a strange aberration in the conversations.

Sessions' analysis is part of a trend in Hume studies that does not see Philo's affirmations in Part 12 as a radical reversal. Badia Cabrera, for instance, notes that Philo's 'apparent turnabout was not, however, completely unexpected' since he agreed with Cleanthes regarding 'the strong impression that the contemplation of the order and uniformity of nature produces in us, which sensibly forces us to assent to theism, or at least to the existence of an intelligent Author of nature.'[27] An older article by William Parent compares the various major assertions of Philo in Part 12 (that the evidence of design in the world increases man's feelings of respect for its author, the significant difference between the nature of humans and the nature of God, and his condemnation of popular religion) with his views on these subjects as expressed in Parts 1–11. Parent concluded that Philo is consistent on all these issues throughout the *Dialogues*.[28]

Dialogues concerning Natural Religion: Philo and True Religion

After Demea's abrupt and startling departure, Philo concedes that he is 'less cautious' on the matters concerning natural religion than on other topics, and, with that introduction, proceeds to affirm his 'unfeigned sentiments' with regard to religion. His positive assertions may raise suspicions that irony is at play, but, at least three reasons can be presented which support the contention that Philo's sentiments are indeed unfeigned. First of all, as I defended already, the content of Philo's assertions in Part 12 is not that different from things he has already said. Second, his triumph over Cleanthes means that he no longer has need of the various skeptical strategies he employed in the debates. The last reason is that the departure of Demea has changed the dynamic of the conversation. The shifting alliances of the three-sided conversation, and Philo's skill at inducing Demea into thinking that they were in deeper agreement than they in fact were, meant that Philo was forced to be subtle and to hide some of his true ideas. Now, however, the one-on-one discussion with Cleanthes allows him to be less cautious. It is time for full disclosure of his true sentiments.

Nelson Pike has also argued against taking Philo's affirmations as ironic, and indicates four reservations that he has against such a reading. 1) Nearly half of Part 12 is very critical of popular, institutionalized religion, which clearly runs against the thesis that Hume had Philo reverse himself to appease his clergy friends. 2) Why would Hume care for his reputation in a work that he intended for posthumous publication? 3) Such a subterfuge would destroy the carefully crafted dramatic tension of the whole work. Could Hume really describe the *Dialogues* as his 'most artful' philosophical production if the ending is a farce? 4) It is dangerous business to accuse Hume of undermining his own work in this way, especially since the support of the argument from design which Philo professes coheres with theses that Hume published under his own name in the *Natural History*.[29]

That Philo's confessions in Part 12 reflect his profound respect for the order in nature and for the very specific inference that it immediately yields of a divine creator is evident from one of his opening speeches of that part:

A purpose, an intention, a design strikes everywhere the most careless, the most stupid thinker; and no man can be so hardened in absurd systems, as at all times to reject it. . . . One great foundation of the Copernican system is the maxim *that nature acts by the simplest methods, and chooses the most proper means to any end*; and astronomers often, without thinking of it, lay this strong foundation of piety and religion. The same thing is observable in other parts of philosophy: And thus all the sciences almost lead us insensibly to acknowledge a first intelligent Author; and their authority is often so much the greater, as they do not directly profess that intention. (DNR 12.2)

It is not necessary to investigate all of Philo's lengthy speeches in Part 12 in order to draw a connection between the theme of true religion developed in the *Natural History* and Philo's affirmations in Part 12. Passages in which Philo affirms the existence of God appear in the following paragraphs: DNR 12.2–4; 12.6–8; 12.15; 12.31–32, and in several of them, Philo uses forceful language to assert his sincerity. He tells Cleanthes that 'no one has a deeper sense of religion impressed on his mind,' (DNR 12.2) which includes a 'veneration for true religion' and an 'abhorrence of vulgar superstitions' in equal measures (DNR 12.9).

Cleanthes objects a bit, noting that 'religion, however corrupted, is still better than no religion at all,' (DNR 12.10) which sets the stage for Philo to expound on what he considers true religion to be. Cleanthes opines that 'the proper office of religion is to regulate the hearts of man, humanize their conduct, infuse the spirit of temperance, order, and obedience' (DNR 12.12). In this speech, Cleanthes reflects the thinking of many people of his days, including a number of the English deists. They believed that the chief importance of religion was the foundation it provided for morality, which necessitated the threat of eternal punishment and the hope of eternal reward. Hume, of course, did not share this opinion, and Philo's critique of religiously based morality sounds like Hume's own position (cf. E IS, 594–595). Philo quickly distinguished 'philosophical and rational' religion from the kind of religion that Cleanthes had described (DNR 12.13).

We must further consider, that philosophers, who cultivate reason and reflection, stand in less need of such motives to keep them under the restraint of morals: And that the vulgar, who alone may need them, are utterly incapable of so pure a religion as represents the Deity to be pleased with nothing but virtue in human behavior. (DNR 12.15)

Philosophical and rational religion, according to Philo, recognizes that virtue is good in its own right, and its followers stand in no need of threats or enticements for proper living. The same reflections that conclude to the existence of a divine creator also comprehend the necessity of moral living on philosophical grounds alone. While Cleanthes tolerates the popular religions, supposing them to provide meaningful aid for societal morality, Philo counters that abuses and injustices result from religious superstition and enthusiasm (DNR 12.16–21). Philosophical religion is different. Its practice is rare, and the number of genuine followers is small.

Philo cites Seneca that 'to know God is to worship him', and then reflects on the implications of this aphorism:

All other worship is indeed absurd, superstitious, and even impious. It degrades him to the low condition of mankind, who are delighted with entreaty, solicitation, presents, and flattery. . . . Nor would any of human race merit his *favor* but a very few, the philosophical theists, who entertain or rather indeed endeavor to entertain suitable notions of his divine perfections. (DNR 12.31–32)

The vulgar religionists suppose that God delights in applause because he possesses passions like their own, while the philosophical theists only assert those qualities which cohere with philosophical reflections on divine perfections. The import of Seneca's aphorism is highlighted if it is reversed – to worship God is to know him. Philo asserts that genuine worship occurs when philosophers discern true knowledge of his existence and nature through discursive thought. This knowledge compels no further responsibilities, such as prayer or rituals. The genuine philosopher requires no guidance from these exercises, nor is true religion bolstered by them.

The stage is now set for Philo's confession, in which he famously summarizes the entirety of natural religion in one tortured sentence:

If the whole of natural theology, as some people seem to maintain, resolves itself into one simple, though somewhat ambiguous, at least undefined proposition, *that the cause or causes of order in the universe probably bear some remote analogy to human intelligence*: If this proposition be not capable of extension, variation, or more particular explication: If it affords no inference that affects human life, or can be the source of any action or forbearance: And if the analogy, imperfect as it is, can be carried no further than to the human intelligence; and cannot be transferred, with any appearance of probability, to the other qualities of the mind: If this really be the case, what can the most inquisitive, contemplative, and religious man do more than give a plain, philosophical assent to the proposition, as often as it occurs; and believe that the arguments, on which it is established, exceed the objections which lie against it? (DNR 12.32)

Some (like Gaskin) have suggested that this affirmation is so highly qualified that precious little is actually asserted.[30] There is in fact some truth to this conclusion, but it is also misleading because most commentators think that this 'single proposition' is the high point of Philo's affirmations. In fact, he has already said much about the nature of true religion, and the effectiveness of the evidence of design on our belief in God. Philo's highly qualified proposition regarding human and divine analogy is not unexpected, given the critique of the Machine Analogy. However, neither is it alone among his affirmations.

It seems to me that the important clauses in this passage are not the ones that contain the 'single proposition', which is so often the focus of attention. Toward the end of this confession, Philo asks rhetorically what can the 'most inquisitive, contemplative and religious man' do, but give his assent to the conclusion that a divine being exists based on the evidence of design, since the evidence for this conclusion exceeds the arguments against it. Remove all the critiques of popular religion, the skeptical objections and all the vagaries of debate and argument that are found in the *Dialogues*, and what remains is this assertion. There is a god, who created all that we see, and the evidence of his existence is written in all that he has done.

This is Philo's conclusion, and, it seems to me that it also is Hume's conclusion, on the basis of these two factors. Given that Philo is the most skeptical of all the interlocutors, his positive assertions at the end of the discussions and debate must be given pride of place as the central thesis of the book as a whole. Philo's affirmation statements in Part 12 assert the existence of God, as did Demea and Cleanthes, but Philo's reflections avoid the problems of the other two. They represent the truth that has emerged from the whole discussion. Additionally, since Philo's conclusion coheres with what is asserted regarding the nature of true religion and genuine theism in the *Natural History*, the most reasonable conclusion is that Hume affirms these things, too.

It is appropriate, however, to consider again the possibility of irony. Insofar as Philo is asserting the existence of a deity on the basis of the evidence for design which serves as the basis for genuine theism, he cannot be ironic, since these are the assertions that he has consistently made. It should be noted that these affirmations have not prevented him from continuing his diatribe against vulgar religion. In the main, therefore, I do not see in Philo's affirmation statements in Part 12 any of the clues that suggest irony, elements like incongruous language or known errors being asserted or statements inconsistent with other claims in Hume.

However, some alarm bells can be sounded at the very end of Part 12. There is something incongruous about Philo's commendation to Pamphilus to be a philosophical skeptic, since it is 'the first and most essential step towards being a sound, believing Christian' (DNR 12.32). Factually, this statement is false, since the most essential step for becoming a Christian is the exercise of faith, not skepticism, as Hume surely knows. It is difficult to know what to make of this statement, without engaging in psychological speculation about Hume's motives. Perhaps the intent was to mollify some of the religious leaders who would be fooled into thinking Hume more orthodox than he really was. If this speculation is true, it would be one of the few times that Hume engaged in private, as opposed to stable, irony. Another strange comment is Pamphilus' assessment that Cleanthes is the victor of the discussion. Surely, this verdict cannot be taken seriously, given Philo's triumph in DNR 10.36. If Hume intends Pamphilus' declaration to be taken ironically, it falls flat and sullies the ending of this masterpiece.

Having come now to the end of the *Dialogues*, it is appropriate to revisit the challenge that Box issued when he asserted that no one has been able to definitively codify what true religion is for Hume.[31] In response, here is one such codification, drawn from the texts that have been analyzed. There exists a true religion, rooted in genuine theism, and it is distinct from the beliefs and practices of the common person. There is also a false, popular religion, which arises out of certain human propensities and is characterized by either superstitious doctrines and rituals or enthusiastic flights of fancy. True religion, which is a species of true philosophy, grows out of the awe that one feels in recognition of the pervasive evidences for design, purpose and order that are apparent in the universe. This evidence, fostered by good education and philosophical rigor, produces immediate impressions of the existence of the divine creator and his transcendent perfections. Popular religion is plagued by fluctuating cycles, in which the vulgar religionists may happen upon some religious truths (such as the belief in one god) in the heat of their enthusiastic exaltations, but these beliefs are only coincidental with true religion. They are not based on discursive thought, and eventually cycle back into superstitious polytheism and idolatry. True religion, being a species of true philosophy, is a rare occurrence and only a small number of people are true religionists. True religion holds to a general, not a particular, providence, and tends towards a view of the deity which emphasizes his otherness and distinctiveness from human beings. True worship of this divine being is nothing more than knowledge of him, and there are no religious duties or other practical consequences that are derived from this belief. Belief in true religion does not lead to a religious foundation for morality, nor a belief in an afterlife. This account summarizes the religious beliefs of David Hume, minus only the fuller picture of the divine nature, which will be supplied in the next chapter.

Objections to Hume's Genuine Theism

This final section will consider some objections that may be offered against the thesis of Hume's genuine theism, as seen in the two famous sections from the First *Enquiry*, namely, Section 10, 'Of Miracles', and Section 11, 'Of a Particular Providence and of a Future State'. A survey of these sections, however, will reveal that the criticisms that Hume makes here with regard to the 'religious hypothesis' are not a repudiation of the true religion that he has described in the *Natural History* and the *Dialogues*. Hume is a vociferous critic of popular religion, with its attendant enthusiasms and superstitions, however, he does not deny the existence of God.

In Section 10, Hume offers his very influential and often-discussed argument against the possibility that one could accrue enough reasonable testimony in order to assent to the occurrence of a miracle. Although his argument (if successful) severely blunts what is generally thought to be one of the more important apologetic weapons, the argument as a whole does not necessarily alter belief in the existence of God. Put another way, the occurrence of a miracle may be an excellent argument for the existence of a miracle-working god, but the nonoccurrence of miracles is not a sufficient basis to conclude that there is no god.

Nevertheless, it is possible to observe in some of Hume's comments in this section ideas which are consistent with the two stories thesis. In EHU 10.2.20, Hume notes that one of the evidences against the veracity of miracles is that they mainly seem to occur among 'ignorant and barbarous nations', which means that they are more likely to be believed in by the vulgar rather than the educated people. This observation suggests that the belief in miracles constitutes a kind of enthusiasm, making it a hallmark of popular religion. Hume never specifically makes this identification, but it is in keeping with his analysis.

Also, when Hume makes his summary judgment on the effect of miracles on religion, it should be noted that he is connecting belief in miracles to a species of false religion.

> But according to the principle here explained, this subtraction [the cancelling of testimony regarding miracles by the testimony of experience], with regard to all popular religions, amounts to an entire annihilation; and therefore we may establish it as a maxim, that no human testimony can have such force as to prove a miracle; and make it a just foundation for any such system of religion. (EHU 10.2.35)

For Hume, belief in the miraculous is sufficient to indicate that the believer follows a vulgar and false religion. A follower of true religion has no need of miracles, and the very notion of a miracle is odious to a true religionist. The reason (as Hume suggests in EHU 10.2.38) is that the miracle is supposed to reveal to us knowledge about the nature of the Almighty which is impossible for us to know. This doctrine of the incomprehensibility of the deity coheres with what both Demea and Philo affirmed, and (more importantly) what the true religionist believes. Thus, the content of Section 10 is not found to be in conflict with these interpretations of Hume's beliefs regarding the existence of god as developed from the *Natural History* and the *Dialogues*.

The next section, entitled 'Of a Particular Providence and a Future State', raises stronger challenges for my thesis, but it is not impossible to reconcile what Hume says here with his doctrine of true religion. The first problem before the interpreter is the presence of another dialogue. This section is purported to be an accurate account of a conversation that Hume had with 'a friend who loves sceptical paradoxes'. Some readers are tempted to suppose that Hume's real thoughts are conveyed by the Friend, to whom 'Hume' serves as a foil.[32] While there is no doubt that Hume can be linked to some of the sentiments expressed by the Friend, it seems the best interpretative course of action is to follow the advice that Hume offers in the first paragraph of the section. He is reporting a conversation with a Friend, who 'advances many principles, of which I can by no means approve' (EHU 11.1). However, as many of his thoughts were 'curious' or philosophically interesting, they seemed worthy of reflection by a broader audience. Thus, just as the discussions themselves seemed to speak best for Hume in the *Dialogues*, there is a similar circumstance here in the *Enquiry*. The device of the dialogue allows him the freedom to entertain some explosive ideas, while ensuring a measure of distance.

However, even if I allow the Friend to speak for Hume, this section can still be reconciled with the interpretation of Hume's genuine theism. Given that some of the most stinging criticisms of the argument from design are offered by 'Hume', those who wish to see Hume as an opponent of theism will have to choose one or the other of these options. If Hume is really the Friend, then the comments of 'Hume' cannot be enlisted. On the other hand, if one sees the dialogue as a whole as speaking for Hume (as I do), then one cannot simply lift lines off the page and attribute them to Hume, without considering the conversation as a whole.

The conversation begins with a discussion of the relative freedom that philosophy historically had enjoyed from 'bigotted jealousy', although the tide now seemed to be changing (EHU 11.2). The earlier, illiterate forms of religion have now produced the 'speculative dogmas of religion', which are more sophisticated and, thus, capable of more direct attack on philosophy than their rather toothless ancestors. This combination of speculative religion and superstition has divided up humankind into two groups: the learned and wise versus the vulgar and illiterate. While this brief account does not exactly mirror the two stories of true religion and vulgar religion, it does call to mind the distinction, and suggests a similar solution to the one indicated in the previous section, namely, that the criticisms leveled against religion in this section are in fact only directed at vulgar religion.

Another important qualifier to any discussion of this part is the expressed intent of the Friend. After he takes up 'Hume's' request that he make a speech for Epicurus, the Friend states twice that he makes the speech only in order to see 'how far such questions concern public interest' (EHU 11.9). The purpose of the exercise of the Epicurean speech is to determine what impact such heretical doctrines (such as a denial of a particular providence and a future state) would have on society. The Friend announces (in a scornful tone) that he will not 'examine the justness' of an argument which concludes to 'such a glorious display of intelligence [which proceeds] from the fortuitous concourse of atoms' (EHU 11.10). This comment is surely ironic, since Epicurus was well-known to have formulated his atomic theory on an atheistic basis. The Friend claims that he does not disbelieve in the existence of god, (EHU 11.11) which may be sincere. It is certainly not implausible (or even difficult) to criticize a particular argument for the existence of God, but still affirm his existence on other bases.

What follows this qualification is a prolonged attack by the Friend on the conclusions of natural religion, especially the reasoning from effects to causes which presumes to be able to determine the nature of the cause. At the heart of the Friend's speech is this passage:

> If you think, that the appearances of things prove such causes, it is allowable for you to draw an inference concerning the existence of these causes. In such complicated and sublime subjects [the religious hypothesis], every one should be indulged in the liberty of conjecture and argument. But here you ought to rest. If you come backward, and arguing from your inferred causes, conclude, that any other fact has existed, or will exist, in the course of nature, which may serve as a fuller display of particular attributes; I must admonish you, that you have departed from the method of reasoning, attached to the present subject, and have certainly added something to the attributes of the cause, beyond what appears in the effect. (EHU 11.18)

The point that the Friend emphasizes is that it *is* permissible to argue from the effect to the existence of a cause. As a general rule, however, one is permitted only to conclude that there is a cause, and may not speculate regarding its nature. The problem, according to the Friend, occurs when one attempts to pursue this kind of reasoning 'backwards' in order to infer something regarding the nature of the deity, solely from an analysis of the effects. This position is reminiscent of Philo's perspective that the evidence for design infers a creator whose nature, unfortunately, is incomprehensible. How much of this point of view is shared by Hume is a question to be taken up in the next chapter. For now, however, it is clear that the existence of a god has not been denied.

The Friend concludes his speech with a set of remarks that ranks among the most pointed of those against religion in all of Hume's corpus:

> While we argue from the course of nature, and infer a particular intelligent cause, which first bestowed, and still preserves order in the universe, we embrace a principle, which is both uncertain and useless. It is uncertain; because the subject lies entirely beyond the reach of human experience. It is useless; because our knowledge of this cause being derived entirely from the course of nature, we can never, according to the rules of just reasoning, return back from the cause with any new inference. (EHU 11.23)

The charge that the existence of a divine creator (the 'particular intelligent cause') is an uncertain and useless principle seems a devastating setback in any attempt to cast Hume as a theist. However, there are some things to keep in mind. It is not necessarily the case that the Friend's comments are to be equated with Hume's beliefs. They may be simply Epicurus' beliefs. The Friend was tasked with voicing his sentiments, which Hume publishes because he believes that they are worthy of consideration.

However, even if the Friend's comments here do genuinely reflect Hume, they are not as trenchant as they might first appear. The Friend really does no more than articulate aspects of Hume's true religion that have been developed already. Is there uncertainty? Yes, because one cannot really know the nature of God. Is the thesis useless? Yes, there are no practical consequences to be discovered from the knowledge that God exists, in terms of moral or religious responsibilities. The charges of uncertainty and uselessness, thus, are really nothing more than what was already observed about Hume's true religion, admittedly expressed in a much more pejorative way.

'Hume' responds at the end of this harangue by asserting, in typically empiricist language, that experience should be our only guide in matters epistemological. He does, however, raise the problem of a half-finished building or a human footprint on the sand, both circumstances which cry out for some explanation (EHU 11.24). The principle of sufficient reason, although not explicitly stated, certainly lies behind this objection, and it points to the necessity of a cause for observed effects. The response of the Friend to 'Hume's' Cleanthes-like perspective parallels Philo's point of view. The Friend rejoins that to reason in this manner regarding the universe and its creator is to overlook that those two entities are singular, and that other members of their genera are not available for inspection and comparison. He says, 'The Deity is known to us only by his productions, and is a single being in the universe, not comprehended under any species or genus, from whose experience attributes or qualities, we can, by analogy, infer any attribute or quality in him' (EHU 11.26). The Friend also reiterates the problem of assuming God's conduct would mirror our own. These comments break no new ground, echoing Philo's critiques of Cleanthes' analogy-based teleology.

A new note is sounded, however, in 'Hume's' final response, which is indeed the last word of this conversation. 'Hume', sounding very much like his namesake, wonders if it is indeed possible 'for a cause to be known only by its effect' (EHU 11.30). It is only when the cause and effect are repeatedly observed together, that one infers the causal relationship because of the constant conjunction of the two items. Since this is not the case with the teleological reasoning from universe to creator, serious questions are raised about this kind of reasoning. 'Hume' specifically does not make this application ('I leave it to your own reflection to pursue the consequences of this principle'). He only articulates the basic principle that experience and observation, being the only guides that we can reasonably trust for making inferences, are not available to us concerning the deity.

This paragraph is probably the closest passage in all of Hume's writing to the conventional story that has been my target. 'Hume' invokes a strict empiricist view, which excludes all entities not available for sensory inspection from being objects of knowledge. Does this text undermine the interpretation that has been presented or derail the thesis that Hume was a theist? In my judgment, it does not, for the following reasons. First, this passage is only relevant as an indication of Hume's true beliefs if 'Hume' speaks for Hume at this point. One cannot give an unqualified affirmative to this question, although it is a plausible point of view. It is, however, also plausible that Hume simply intends this perspective to be part of the general debate and discussion regarding the possible insights of natural religion.

Even, however, if one judges that it is more likely that 'Hume' here speaks for Hume, it is not at all clear that this passage overturns the many texts and passages that have already been cited which support the thesis that Hume was a theist. This passage ends on a note of skepticism, but in many other places, Hume writes with confidence, and even awe, regarding the overwhelming evidence of design that is found throughout the world, which cries out for some creator. Despite the possibility that this passage indicates some doubts on the part of Hume regarding the existence of a deity, I believe that the most persuasive interpretation is that Hume is rounding out the give and take of a philosophical conversation, and laying out the options for the reader to consider. It is not, in my judgment, an indication of doubts or agnosticism on Hume's part, especially when balanced against the great number of affirmation texts that has been presented.

I hold a similar perspective about the passage that closes the first *Enquiry*, in which Hume writes with some heat that if we discover any volumes of 'divinity or school metaphysics' which do not exhibit abstract reasoning regarding mathematics, or does not follow the empirical approach, we ought to 'commit it then to the flames' (EHU 12.3.34). This passage, frankly, contains more rhetoric than pure analysis. Hume's own works do not meet the criterion that he lays out. His works contain abstract reasonings regarding the nature of causality, the problem of knowing and, of course, the nature of true religion, not to mention a host of other metaphysical concerns. Hume is really not an opponent of metaphysics, but rather an opponent of irresponsible or excessive metaphysics, as has been repeatedly exemplified throughout this chapter. Therefore, this passage does not, I believe, pose serious threats to my thesis regarding Hume's advocacy of true religion and the existence of a divine being.

I close this chapter with a final affirmation statement from Hume. In a 1743 letter to a friend, Hume critiques a sermon he heard from a Mr. Leechman, and playfully wishes that Leechman would answer his objection to the need for religious devotion and prayer, 'and indeed to every thing we commonly call Religion, except the Practice of Morality, and the Assent of the Understanding to the Proposition *that God exists*' (L 21; 1.50). Even in private letters, the consistent testimony throughout the Humean corpus is that he affirms the existence of a divine being. In letters, essays and philosophical treatises, he retains his belief in the god of true religion, despite the sharp criticisms that he brings against so many aspects of false and popular religion. To fail to recognize these affirmations is to severely misunderstand one of the fundamental elements in Hume's philosophy of religion.

Chapter 5

Hume on the Nature of God

Hume's God

The tone for a discussion of the nature of Hume's theism was set a long time ago by Thomas Huxley in his 1879 book entitled *Hume*. After citing Philo's final confession in Part 12, Huxley offers this assessment:

> Such being the sum total of Hume's conclusion, it cannot be said that his theological burden is a heavy one. But, if we turn from the *Natural History of Religion*, to the *Treatise*, the *Inquiry*, and the *Dialogues*, the story of what happened to the ass laden with salt, who took to the water, irresistibly suggests itself. Hume's theism, such as it is, dissolves away in the dialectic river, until nothing is left but the verbal sack in which it was contained.[1]

Huxley's sarcasm notwithstanding, he correctly observes that Hume does affirm the existence of a divine being, as was shown in the previous chapter. Huxley's colorful remarks do raise a significant question, however. What kind of character does Hume's deity possess? What kind of a being does Hume imagine him to be? If the conventional story is true, then the project of investigating Hume's viewpoint on the nature of God is, at most, a short, uninteresting endeavor. In fact, I believe that the opposite is true. Not only have I shown that Hume is a theist and that he affirmed belief in a true religion, I also think that a meaningful and substantial inquiry can be made into the nature of Hume's God, and that study is the thesis of this chapter.

In all of Hume's texts, he affirms the existence of God, and never claims an atheistic perspective. Capaldi categorically asserts that 'Hume never denied the existence of God. In none of his writings does Hume say or imply that he does not accept the existence of God.'[2] In the previous chapter, I made the case for Hume's genuine theism, and concluded with a codification of Hume's religious belief, which is, however, incomplete. It is necessary to append to that statement what Hume thinks of the *nature* of the god of true, philosophical religion.

Specifically, I will be addressing these three issues regarding the nature of the deity, from which will emerge a fairly complete picture of the nature of Hume's God (so far as he presents it). These issues are the extent to which the divine may be known or understood, the nature of the deity's providence, and whether there is divine moral goodness. A final, concluding section will consider how best to characterize or name Hume's theism.

On Divine Knowability

Early on in the *Dialogues*, Cleanthes and Demea engage in a bit of name-calling, which brings into sharp relief this problem of divine knowability. After the presentation of Cleanthes' Machine Analogy, both Philo and Demea present strenuous objections. Demea's main complaint is that it makes the deity too similar to humankind.

> His ways are not our ways. His attributes are perfect, but incomprehensi-
> ble . . . it must be acknowledged that, by representing the Deity as so
> intelligible and comprehensible, and so similar to a human mind, we are
> guilty of the grossest and most narrow partiality, and make our selves the
> model of the whole universe. (DNR 3.11–12)

Demea's point of view emphasizes the otherness of the deity, who is utterly different from human beings in both the quality and degree of his attributes. In their perfection, his attributes are so far beyond any human characteristics that may bear the same name (for example, love and intelligence) that they do not even remotely mean the same thing, with the result that the nature of God is wholly inscrutable. Demea insists on a complete equivocation of any term applied both to humans and God, arguing that any analogy between divine and human characteristics is tantamount to creating the Creator in our own image.

Cleanthes seizes on this extreme position and immediately exposes its main disadvantage:

> The Deity, I can readily allow, possesses many powers and attributes of
> which we can have no comprehension: But, if our ideas, so far as they go,
> be not just and adequate, and correspondent to his real nature, I know
> not what there is in this subject worth insisting on. Is the name, without
> any meaning, of such mighty importance? Or how do you *mystics*, who
> maintain the absolute incomprehensibility of the Deity, differ from
> sceptics or atheists, who assert that the first cause of All is unknown and
> unintelligible? (DNR 4.1)

If the same word is used of humans and the divine in a completely equivocal manner, Cleanthes argues, then that word is simply an empty term, devoid of any signification. This position is no better than some anti-intellectual mysticism or agnosticism or, worst of all, atheism, since not only does it deny any real knowledge of God's character, it also eschews any knowledge of a first cause. There is no practical difference between this position and the assertion that no god initiated the universe, since neither provide any kind of tangible, substantial answer to the question. Cleanthes calls this *mysticism* and Demea a mystic, presumably in the hopes of shaming Demea into rethinking his position.

Surprisingly, Demea gladly accepts the moniker, and reiterates his opposition to any notion of an analogy between God and persons. He, in turn, has a nickname for Cleanthes. He is an *anthropomorphite*, that is, one who cannot get beyond his own humanity in the attempt to conceptualize an entirely other being. Cleanthes constructs his deity out of fundamentally human attributes, and this act, Demea charges, is heresy.

It is important to note that there are actually two aspects of this disagreement, one of them epistemological and the other metaphysical. The epistemological question concerning the degree to which the deity is knowable or discoverable. What kind of knowledge is available regarding the nature of the deity? The answer to this question, however, depends on the response to the metaphysical problem, which is, how much is the divine being like or unlike us? Is there anything in his character which resembles our own? Although it is clear that the nature of the divine being informs the degree to which he is knowable, it is also true that the degree to which he is knowable suggests what his nature is. Thus, the questions are linked. If God is wholly unknowable, then he is wholly different. However, if he is knowable in some way, then it follows that he is analogous to us in some way.

An early indication of how difficult it was for Hume to work through these metaphysical and epistemological issues comes in this letter to William Mure:

It must be acknowledg'd that Nature has given us a strong Passion of Admiration for whatever is excellent, & of Love & Gratitude for whatever is benevolent & beneficial, & that the Deity possesses these Attributes in the highest Perfection & yet I assert that he is not the natural Object of any Passion or Affection. He is no Object either of the Senses or Imagination, & very little of the Understanding, without which it is impossible to excite any Affection. A remote Ancestor, who left us Estates & Honours, acquir'd with Virtue, is a great Benefactor, & yet 'tis impossible to bear him any Affection, because unknown to us; tho in general we know him to be a Man or a human Creature, which brings him vastly nearer our Comprehension than an invisible infinite Spirit. (L 21; 1.51)

Anders Jeffner recognizes the interplay between two theological perspectives in the *Dialogues*, and speculates on which position ultimately wins Hume's approval. Jeffner observes that there are two mindsets which the three interlocutors sometimes display – and also observed in the letter above – the *aspect of similarity* and the *aspect of mystery*.[3] The aspect of similarity suggests that the attributes of God are perfected versions of the same attributes that one observes in humans. Clearly, this point of view corresponds with Cleanthes' anthropomorphism. The aspect of mystery holds that the divine is fundamentally unknowable and unlike human persons, which, of course, is linked to the mysticism that one finds in the characters of Demea and (sometimes) Philo.

Since each of these perspectives tends toward an extreme, each is also prone to a kind of dissatisfaction. The religious person expects a degree of reverence and complexity in the notion of God which is difficult to articulate. If there is not some measure of transcendence in our understanding of the divine being, then that conception is found wanting. On the other hand, if one overemphasizes the transcendent inexplicability, then one runs the risk of emptiness, in which what is articulated of God actually has no content and no meaning.[4]

Thus, the anthropomorphism of Cleanthes is subject to the problem of not meeting the criterion of transcendent inexplicability, while the mysticism of Demea is in danger of being devoid of any meaningful insight into the nature of God. According to Jeffner, the dilemma of these extreme points of view is that, for Hume, it is impossible to defend any view of God's nature that is in agreement with Christian orthodoxy.[5] This judgment notwithstanding, it is worthwhile to examine which of the horns of the dilemma (similarity or mystery) Hume ultimately chooses.

To pursue this question, it is necessary to revisit the first half of the *Natural History*, where Hume first makes his distinction between true religion and popular or false religion. He observes that false religion is characterized by a tendency towards belief in many gods (NHR 2.2), which in turn leads to the superstitious belief that these local deities control the 'fortuitous accidents' of life (NHR 3.3). The belief that these powers control things like the weather and the small happenstances of life is nothing more than a belief in a particular providence, an assent which occurs when this natural tendency to deify inexplicable circumstances is not counterbalanced by solid education in the sciences and philosophy (NHR 5.2 and 6.1–2).

On the other hand, true religion, which is rooted in true philosophy, will lead to a much different conception of the nature of the divine force that lies behind all that we observe. First of all, the true religionist will affirm a general providence instead of a particular providence, an aspect of the divine activity that I will explore in the next section of this chapter. Secondly, however, Hume indicates that those who hold to the true religion realize that the evidence of design and order in the universe can only properly lead to the determination that there is but *one* designer.

> Were men led into the apprehension of invisible, intelligible power by a contemplation of the works of nature, they could never possibly entertain any conception but of a single being, who bestowed existence and order on this vast machine, and adjusted all its parts, according to one regular plan or connected system. . . . All things in the universe are evidently of a piece. Every thing is adjusted to every thing. One design prevails throughout the whole. And this uniformity leads the mind to acknowledge one author. (NHR 2.2)

In the first part of the *Natural History*, Hume mentions the traditional transcendent characteristics of the deity in his comments on the natural progression of our human thinking regarding the divine nature.

> We may as reasonably imagine, that men inhabited palaces before huts and cottages, or studied geometry before agriculture; as assert that the Deity appeared to them a pure spirit, omniscient, omnipotent and omnipresent, before he was apprehended to be a powerful, though limited being, with human passions and appetites, limbs and organs. (NHR 1.5)

Hume does not assert, at this point, that true religion holds that the Deity possesses these transcendental attributes, but rather says that these would not be the first conceptions that humans would discover about God. Throughout the *Natural History*, Hume is reluctant to use the traditional theological terms about God (the omni-prefixed words), and it seems reasonable to conclude that he has in mind the tension between the aspects of similarity and mystery. To use such language, however, is to incline towards the anthropomorphic side of the debate.

The specific language that Hume repeatedly uses, however, in describing the nature of God in the *Natural History*, has to do with power and intelligence. From time to time, Hume uses very general language to speak of the deity – 'the supreme being' or the 'perfect being', which can be difficult to specify. The phrases 'supreme being' or 'supreme God' or 'supreme deity' are found in NHR 1.7, 4.1, 6.1, 14.6 and 15.6, and Hume speaks of the 'perfect being' in NHR 6.5. These general terms could potentially be understood in various ways: superiority and/or perfection in terms of morality, or power, or knowledge or all of these things. Given that Hume names the deity supreme more often than perfect, it seems that the perfection of the deity should be understood more in terms of perfect or complete power. Hume also mentions divine omnipotence in NHR 6.1 and the 'Sovereign mind' in NHR 6.2. Thus, it seems that the transcendent attribute which Hume is most comfortable asserting of God is his omnipotence, and I take the phrase 'supreme being' to be referring to the superior power of the Almighty.

In many instances, however, Hume clearly indicates his assent that this supreme spiritual being is intelligent and powerful by referring to him as the 'invisible, intelligent power'. Passages where Hume uses this phrase are found in these paragraphs from the NHR 2.2, 2.5, 3.2, 3.4, 4.1, 5.2 and 15.5. In the Introduction, Hume speaks of an 'intelligent author', and he used the phrase 'invisible spiritual intelligence' in NHR 5.9. Throughout the affirmation texts in the *Natural History*, Hume specifically refers to the intelligence of the first cause and also to the great power that is required to create everything and initiate the laws of general providence, and he was careful not to mention other traditionally divine characteristics (like holiness and love). Thus, his references to the perfection of the deity should not be read in a Scholastic manner, inferring various moral perfections, but only those transcendent features associated with power and intelligence.

What are the implications of the fact that Hume's god is supreme in power and intelligence? Undoubtedly, this deity is the first cause and creator of all. Hume asserts these designations on numerous occasions (NHR Introduction, 2.2, 4.1, 5.2, 6.1–2, 6.5, 15.1, 15.5–6). Hume does not examine in detail the exact nature of this power or intelligence. Scholastics like Aquinas gave close attention to the outworking of these ideas, but Hume does little beyond acknowledging that the deity possesses transcendental power and intelligence.

The most significant implication is that the very act of allowing these designations means that Hume is not wholeheartedly embracing the mystical stance. He is willing, with qualifications, to assert that the deity is knowable, specifically, he is one, he fills the roles of creator and first cause, and, further, that to do so requires surpassing intelligence and power. Hume retained doubts regarding the overly optimistic conclusion of many natural theologians (including the English deists and also his more theologically orthodox contemporaries, like Butler or Clarke or Locke) who believed that more can be known of the deity than Hume thought could be justified. Thus, while Hume does conclude that the deity is knowable in the *Natural History*, on the whole, he is much more cautious than most regarding the degree to which the divine is knowable. These conclusions will be borne out as this investigation returns to the *Dialogues* and the debate between anthropomorphism and mysticism.

While Cleanthes and Demea were waging the debate between mysticism and anthropomorphism, Philo usually sided with Demea, although his support for the mystics was soft. Pamphilus observed that his support of Demea in DNR 2.25 was vehement, but 'somewhat between jest and earnest'. So, it is not a surprise when Philo drops the facade and tries to minimize the difference between the anthropomorphic and mystical positions. He suggests that the difference between these two positions is more verbal than substantial. He says that there is really no difference between saying that the deity is God or Mind or Thought, favoring slightly the anthropomorphic side (DNR 12.6).

He continues by subjecting hypothetical theists and atheists to a round of questions. He would ask the theist if there is not a 'great and immeasurable, because incomprehensible, difference between the *human* and *divine* mind'. The more pious he is, the more he will agree. But to the atheist, Philo will ask about the great coherence and sympathy that exists among all the elements of the universe. Do not all these things bear a remote analogy to each other? Philo asserts that no atheist can deny it and then presses for the further concession that 'the principle which first arranged and still maintains order' bears a resemblance to human thought. This admission he also secures. Thus, Philo concludes, the difference between the two positions is negligible.

The theist allows that the original intelligence is very different from human reason: The atheist allows that the original principle of order bears some remote analogy to it. Will you quarrel, Gentlemen, about the degrees, and enter into a controversy which admits not of any precise meaning, nor consequently of any determination? If you should be so obstinate, I should not be surprised to find you insensibly change sides; while the theist on the one hand exaggerates the dissimilarity between the supreme Being and frail, imperfect, variable, fleeting, and mortal creatures; and the atheist on the other magnifies the analogy among all the operations of nature, in every period, every situation, and every position. Consider then, where the real point of controversy lies, and if you cannot lay aside your disputes, endeavor, at least, to cure yourselves of your animosity. (DNR 12.7)

Ultimately, Philo judges that the dispute can be mediated. There is a kind of analogy that exists between the human and the divine. This metaphysical similarity is clear from all the evidence of creation. Thus, the answer to the debate is that a mitigated aspect of similarity is affirmed. If there is some slight analogy, then it follows that the deity is knowable. Philo's challenge to the atheist on this point is entirely in keeping with the conclusions of true religion that have been highlighted throughout the *Natural History* and the *Dialogues*.

What settles the debate, however, is the bold move Hume makes that other theists will not, to wit, that the god of Hume's true religion is not a perfectly moral being. At this point the analogy of metaphysical similarity breaks down. Cleanthes' Machine Analogy falters, according to Hume, not because it fails to give adequate grounds for a supreme deity, but because it fails to give adequate grounds for a supremely *moral* deity. Why Hume's god cannot be moral will be explored after the question of divine providence is investigated, but what should be observed at this point is that the denial of the divine goodness means that the question of transcendent inexplicability is completely revised. It is no longer necessary to preserve it in order to maintain the need for worship. Hume's god requires (and deserves) no worship. The inexplicability that remains (for instance, regarding the exact nature of his power or intelligence) simply results from the paltry experience we have of the divine being.

On Divine Providence

This next point in this investigation into the nature of Hume's theism is something that, while, frequently mentioned by Hume, is, nevertheless, not well understood by contemporary readers. The topic is divine providence, and specific debate is the distinction between *particular providence* and *general providence*. Hume was a frequent critic of particular providence, which in turn provoked censure by the theologians and clergy of his day, who maintained a strong view of divine providence. What is frequently misconstrued is the difference between the two perspectives and what Hume meant in acknowledging a general providence. The distinction may seem obscure to modern ears, but it was a sharp point of debate in the 18th century. Some theological and historical context is needed.

Since the time of the Protestant Reformation, the providence of God has been understood to encompass three specific aspects of divine activity. First, there is *Preservation*, which refers to the act of maintaining and sustaining the created universe. The second aspect is known as *Concurrence*, which is the cooperation of God in all things and events, by directing them according to their individual properties. The third aspect is known as *Governance*, and this aspect of providence marks out the divine direction of all events in order to achieve his purposes.[6] Although ideas of divine providence are found in the Old Testament and also in the thought of the Stoics, the fully developed notion of providence is credited to the Protestant Reformers and specifically John Calvin.[7]

These three aspects are all evident in a definition offered by John Leland, the conservative Irish minister who published several editions of his book *A View of the Principal Deistical Writers* in the 1750s.

> By the doctrine of providence I understand the doctrine of an All-Perfect Mind, preserving and governing the vast universe in all its parts, presiding over the creatures, especially rational, moral agents, inspecting their conduct, and superintending and ordering the events relating to them, in the best and fittest manner, with infinite wisdom, righteousness, and equity.[8]

The first two aspects of divine providence indicate the ways by which God provides guidance to the universe as an outgrowth of the original creative act. It is by the use of secondary causes that God exercises his providence over the universe in concurring and preserving. As the first cause, he set in motion the course of events which results in such things as our bodies being nourished by the food we eat and the environment being maintained by rainfall and sunlight. These secondary causes are under his direction, since they are the means by which he sustains and preserves the universe. Additionally, these events also reflect his ongoing concurrence, since, as an active deity, he cooperates and participates in all causal activity.

The third aspect of divine providence, however, indicates a heightened and direct role for God in the events of the world, and so the governance element of providence has always been the most controversial. Governance is that part of divine providence whereby he intervenes in the affairs of the world to do things like answer prayers, perform miracles or send natural disasters that specifically impact the lives of individual persons. In short, it refers to the divine prerogative to reward or to punish according to his purposes for human individuals. The extent to which God acts in this way was the source of controversies in Hume's day, as it is in ours.

It is the governance of God that is associated with particular providence, as is highlighted by Leland, who offers a description of just what it is:

> And now it appears what is to be understood by the doctrine of a particular providence. It signifies, that providence extends its care to the particulars or individuals of the human race, . . . that God exerciseth a continual inspection over them, and knoweth and observeth both the good and evil actions they perform, and even the most secret affections and dispositions of their heart; that he observeth them not merely as an unconcerned spectator, who is perfectly indifferent about them, but as the Supreme Ruler and Judge, so as to govern them with infinite wisdom in a way consistent with their moral agency, and to reward or punish them in the properest manner, and in the fittest season.[9]

As Leland points out, it is ultimately the intervening activity of God, based on the inspection and observation of righteous or sinful activity, that is God's particular providence towards individuals. These particular activities are an application of the general plan of God, carried out in the lives of each person.

The distinction between general and particular providence is present in this passage from Calvin's *Institutes*:

> At the outset, then, let my readers grasp that providence means not that by which God idly observes from heaven what takes place on earth, but that by which, as keeper of the keys, he governs all events. . . . Whence it follows that providence is lodged in the act; for many babble too ignorantly of bare foreknowledge. Not so crass is the error of those who attribute a governance to God, but of a confused and mixed sort, as I have said, namely, one that by a general motion revolves and drive the system of the universe, with its several parts, but which does not specifically direct the action of the individual creatures.[10]

According to Calvin, general providence refers to the God's guidance over the universe in accordance with his universal plans and laws inaugurated at creation. Particular providence, on the other hand, Calvin argues, refers to God's direct involvement with the human community, which includes things like punishing the wicked, answering prayer or strengthening the faithful by testing their faith. Roughly speaking, general providence corre-lates to concurrence, while particular providence is one articulation of divine governance.[11]

This distinction is expressed by the Friend in the debate he has with 'Hume' in the first *Enquiry*, although he argues the reverse of Calvin.

I deny a providence, you say, and supreme governor of the world, who guides the course of events, and punishes the vicious with infamy and dis-appointment, and rewards the virtuous with honour and successes, in all their undertaking. But surely, I deny not the course itself of events, which lies open to every one's enquiry and examination. . . . And if you affirm, that, while a divine providence is allowed, and a supreme distributive justice in the universe, I ought to expect some more particular reward for the good, and punishment of the bad, beyond the ordinary course of events. (EHU 11.20)

This theological context is helpful in understanding the complex debate regarding providence in the 17th and 18th century Great Britain. There was a growing disquiet among some of the English intellectuals with the notion that God exercises a particular providence in his dealings with peo-ple. Their unease existed on a number of levels. On a theological level, some church leaders and religious scholars, like Thomas Sprat and John Spencer,[12] raised the question that God's special intervention seemed unfair or unseemly. To them, it seemed undignified that God would set aside his general laws to act specifically in some cases. It suggested that his original course of action was insufficient or poorly planned. Others raised the difficulty of discerning just when God acted particularly, that is, in answer to prayer or to perform a miracle. Perhaps things happened simply according to their normal course or the plan already laid out. Lastly, the doctrine of particular providence gave rise to enthusiasms and fanaticisms, as the faithful believed themselves to have a unique relationship with God or special insight into his dealings. The result was private illuminations, superstitions like astrology and magic, and fanatical visions, all detested by the elite.[13]

Among the intellectuals, the tendency was to see Newtonian mechanical philosophy and experimental science as alleviating the need for any partic-ular providence, since all things could (potentially) be explained in terms of the newly discovered laws of physics. It would be a long time for the scientific community to become fully secular, but a first step was the move away from particular providence. Finally, there was a middle ground staked out by those like Henry More, Ralph Cudworth and Robert Boyle who held that a belief in a particular providence was necessary to appreciate Newton's discoveries of the wonders of the natural world.

> Only a continually active Providence could explain so well made and con-
> tinually well functioning a device [as nature]. For many learned English
> people, Newton's hypothesis of universal gravitation satisfied any poten-
> tial conflict between God's extraordinary and ordinary providential
> interventions. His theory of gravity allowed itself to be interpreted as a
> proof of the continual interventions of God in the operation of the
> world.[14]

It is against the backdrop of this debate that Hume's reflections on the role of God in the world should be considered. He stands with those of his day who had severe reservations about particular providence. His critique of miracles and disdain for enthusiasms go hand-in-hand with his unease regarding particular providence. However, as he points out in *A Letter from a Gentleman*, the rejection of a particular providence does not mean that he rejects any role for God in the world. Deism (popularly understood) need not be raised here, since the historical English deists of Hume's age were divided over the extent to which divine providence operates. The rather simplistic notion of popular deism provides only for a first-cause deity, who wound things up and let them go. The notion of general providence stands somewhere in between the extremes of the absentee god of popular deism and the hyperactive god of particular providence. Hume stood in good company with many of the intellectuals of his day who rejected Calvin's version of God's providence and were more willing to entertain a view in which God does not control every detail.

Hume's rejection of particular providence was, however, one of the rea-sons that some of his contemporaries accused him of atheism, costing him a professorship and leading him to compose *A Letter from a Gentleman to His Friend in Edinburgh*. Hume's *Letter* is intended to show that he objected only to the brand of providence he found in continental thinkers like Descartes and Malebrache. He does not specifically endorse general providence in the *Letter*, but argues against the occasionalism that was characteristic of the Cartesian school. *Occasionalism* was the belief that causal events, like a fire burning a log or food nourishing a person, happened because God inter-vened at every occasion to bring about the requisite effect. In other words, the causal activity of things in the world was always due to the direct inter-vention of God and not to the regular laws of physics implemented at creation. Hume argued that his position coheres with both the ancient philosophers and the Scholastics, and that it was the Cartesians who are out of step with traditional views of providence.

> No one, till *Des Cartes* and *Malebranche*, ever entertained an Opinion that Matter had no Force either *primary* or *secondary*, and *independent* or *concurrent*, and could not so much as properly be called an *Instrument* in the Hands of the Deity, to serve any of the Purposes of Providence. These Philosophers last-mentioned substituted the Notion of *occasional Causes*, by which it was asserted that a Billiard Ball did not move another by its Impulse, but was only the Occasion why the Deity, in pursuance of general Laws, bestowed Motion on the second Ball. (LG 28)

It is not necessary to discuss all the questions raised by the *Letter*, such as, whether Hume was being ironic or duplicitous in associating himself with the Scholastics (perhaps) or whether his historical analysis of the doctrine of providence is accurate (probably not). What is to the point is that Hume was certainly correct that his denial of particular providence in favor of general providence did not make him an atheist, nor did it take him out of the broad mainstream of contemporary theological discussions regarding divine providence. Nothing in Hume's position negates divine preservation or concurrence, and it is possible that Hume believed in some weakened notion of divine governance, although this conjecture cannot be established from what Hume has written.

Hume's continued defense of the notion of general providence can also be observed, interestingly enough, in several of his more controversial essays in which he challenges some cherished religious doctrines and beliefs. That he can affirm general providence, and even use it as part of his critique of popular religion, is evidence that his espousal of general providence is not to be seen as ironic. It is a vital aspect of the true religion, which exists under the umbrella of true philosophy. The pieces to be considered in this vein include the scandalous essays 'Of Suicide' and 'Of the Immortality of the Soul', plus the less contentious 'Of the Original Contract'.

Hume's fullest treatment of the nature of general providence came in 'Of Suicide', a once-suppressed essay intended to show that suicide is not criminal or immoral. Hume began by showing that the arguments that suicide is criminal are all faulty. Thus, suicide can only be wrong if it is a transgression of a duty to God, to our neighbor, or to ourselves (E Su, 580). The topic of general providence arose in the consideration of divine duties. Hume argued that the 'almighty creator' established immutable laws which govern the material world and gave to all living creatures 'bodily and mental powers' by which they regulate their lives. The result is that 'the providence of the deity appears not immediately in any operation, but governs every thing by those general and immutable laws, which have been established from the beginning' (E Su, 581). The effect of these laws is that all events are, therefore, the result of divine action and those creatures which he has endowed with the ability to cause effects. Hume affirmed a compatibilist approach to the problem of free will. An effect occurs both as a result of the deity's general providence – the laws which govern the inanimate world – as well as the powers given to living beings.

> A house, which falls by its own weight, is not brought to ruin by his providence more than one destroyed by the hands of men; nor are the human faculties less his workmanship than the laws of motion and gravitation. When the passions play, when the judgment dictates, when the limbs obey; this is all the operation of God; and upon these animate principles, as well as upon the inanimate, has he established the government of the universe. (E Su, 581)

Since the cause of actions is traced to both the initial providence of God, as well as the more immediate inanimate or animate causes, there are no effects that are solely the responsibility of the deity, like a miracle or some kind of divine intervention which overrides the natural flow which results from the immutable laws. It is here that Hume makes the point that suicide is not a transgression of a duty we have to God. It is false, Hume argues, to assert that 'the Almighty has reserved to himself, in any peculiar manner, the disposal of the lives of men, and has not submitted that event, in common with others, to the general laws, by which the universe is governed' (E Su, 582). God does not make a special decree to bring to an end the life of a person. If a person dies in a hurricane or as the result of a snakebite or in war or by his own hand, these are all actions that can be traced directly to some inanimate or animate creature and indirectly back to the original implementation of the immutable laws governing all of creation. Put another way, suicide cannot be a transgression of God's plans, since God's plans are to allow living beings to make the decisions that they make. To suggest that God ordains the day of death is to infer that he violates his own original providential law. 'Divine providence is still inviolate, and placed far beyond the reach of human injuries' (E Su, 584).

What does this articulation of general providence reveal about the nature of the divine being? First of all, Hume's portrayal is of a god rather unconcerned about sin. Theologically, the view that all actions – even immoral ones – are part of the original plan of God is problematic since it excuses any sin as simply the result of divine providence. This aspect of his argument would not meet with the approval of any Christian theologian, but it does cohere with Hume's view of the divine morality.

Second, Hume's general providence reveals again a deity who created the universe out of his surpassing power and in accord with his great intelligence. The fact that he does not engage in particular providence means that his ongoing actions are not available for inspection. There is still an element of the inscrutable regarding the nature of God, but his power and intelligence are still evident. The essay 'Of the Original Contract' raises the possibility of other divine attributes that result from general providence.

In 'Of the Original Contract', Hume considers two rival accounts for the justification of government. There is one theory that government can be 'traced up' to the Deity, who intended it as part of his plan of providence, but this theory is countered by those who suppose that human government originated in a tacit agreement by the people who realized that by installing a human king or leader, their lives and interests would be protected. Hume allows that both systems are 'just' and 'prudent', but neither is entirely correct as presented (E OC, 466). Hume's correction of the first theory is revelatory concerning his view of the deity:

> That the DEITY is the ultimate author of all government, will never be denied by any, who admit a general providence, and allow, that all events in the universe are conducted by an uniform plan, and directed to *wise purposes*. As it is impossible for the human race to subsist, at least in any comfortable or secure state, without the protection of government; this institution must certainly have been intended by that *beneficent Being*, who means the good of all his creatures: And as it has universally, in fact, taken place, in all countries, and all ages; we may conclude, with still greater certainty, that it was intended by that *omniscient Being*, who can never be deceived by any event or operation. (E OC, 466, italics added)

Given what has already been seen about the nature of Hume's general providence, his correction of the view that human government can be 'traced up' directly to God is not unexpected. In an ultimate sense, government is the result of God's providence, but only his 'concealed and universal' providence. No ruler can claim more or less of God's favor than another.

The particulars of human government are rooted in human decisions, and not in any particular divine plan.

What is more relevant for this discussion are the qualifiers that Hume used to describe the God behind this general providence, which are italicized in the text above. This divine being operates according to 'wise purposes' and is 'beneficent' and 'omniscient'. Hume specifically described God intending good things for his creatures and, thus, ordering the universe in accordance with his attendant wisdom and goodness. There are, however, some good reasons to question whether Hume truly meant what he says here regarding the good intents and beneficent desires of the deity. These issues will be explored further in the next section, but Hume could not have been entirely truthful in this passage, given what he claimed elsewhere. However, even if Hume was being duplicitous in naming God beneficent, it is clear that he is not being ironic is his assertion of a kind of theocratic view of human government. Thus, Hume's general providence produces human government in keeping with divine wisdom and omniscience, a view which is quite distinct from popular deism.

The issue of general providence is raised briefly in the essay 'Of the Immortality of the Soul', which is similar in many ways to 'Of Suicide'. Not only do both essays challenge deeply held religious beliefs and convictions, with the result that they were suppressed during Hume's lifetime, but they also employ a similar sort of argumentative strategy. Hume sought to undercut the arguments given for the immortality of the soul in the hope that, if successful, there will be no good reasons to give one's assent to that doctrine. In the opening lines, he asserted that the arguments for the eternality of the soul are either metaphysical, moral or natural in nature (E IS, 590). For my purposes, the relevant argument is the second, that it is due to God's justice that human souls survive the death of the body. The true reward for the virtuous and the rightful penalty to the unjust can only be distributed in a life to come, thus the necessity for an eternal soul. This argument is one that was commonly made in Hume's era, both by English deists and orthodox theologians, and it is one of the distinctive features of the notion of particular providence.

> But these arguments are grounded on the supposition, that God has attributes beyond what he has exerted in this universe, with which alone we are acquainted. Whence do we infer the existence of these attributes? It is very safe for us to affirm, that, whatever we know the deity to have actually done, is best; but it is very dangerous to affirm, that he must always do what to us seems best. (E IS, 592)

Again, one may observe that Hume is willing to affirm those attributes of God which are observable (presumably his intelligence and power), but he is reluctant to go further regarding characteristics like justice. There are no empirical grounds on which to propose any notion of God's moral attributes, unlike the evidence for design from which one may infer his transcendental attributes. Hume reiterates his point that God's justice is unknowable.

> As every effect implies a cause, and that another, till we reach the first cause of all, which is the *Deity;* every thing, that happens, is ordained by him; and nothing can be the object of his punishment or vengeance. By what rule are punishments and rewards distributed? What is the divine standard of merit and demerit? (E IS, 594)

It is clear, Hume argues, that divine providence stands behind every cause and effect that we observe. From this fact, we can infer that the deity is a being of power and intelligence, who employs these attributes in the supervision of the world. However, one may not conclude that there is divine justice or any other moral sentiment. There is simply no evidence of such things. Thus, the discussion of general providence leads directly into an investigation of divine morality, which is the topic of the next section.

On Divine Goodness

Traditionally, divine attributes are divided into those that are transcendent and those that are moral. Thus far, it has been evident that Hume has allowed only for the former in the deity of his true religion. These qualities include intelligence, power, a minimal knowability and a general providence. What is overdue for consideration is whether there are any virtues in Hume's God. To answer this question, it is necessary to return to Parts 10 and 11 of the *Dialogues,* where the interlocutors discuss the problem of evil. Hume has his characters present some very difficult challenges to the traditional view that the divine being has infinite goodness and holiness in a manner parallel to his infinite power and intelligence.

Part 10 opens with Demea and Philo commiserating on the suffering that exists in the world and noting that this suffering compels people to worship God. This conversation is suspicious on several levels. First of all, like the calm before the storm, Cleanthes is noticeably silent. Secondly, readers of the *Natural History* will recognize that this religious response to suffering is a species of superstitious religion. It is an attempt to mollify an angry deity through meaningless ritual. That Philo should praise such a circumstance is indeed dubious, and it is not long before his true colors show. When Cleanthes finally speaks, the real discussion begins.

The shortness of Cleanthes' speech at DNR 10.20 belies its impact. He allows that while others may feel that there is evil in the world, he confesses that 'I feel little or nothing of it in myself, and hope that it is not so common as you represent it.' Cleanthes' denial of the existence of human misery in the world brings a sharp, surprised response from Philo, for whom the presence of suffering in the world seems self-evident. Philo realizes, however, what motivates Cleanthes' position, and it is the desire to affirm the goodness of God on the basis of the Machine Analogy.

The Machine Analogy employs a comparison of the characteristics of the world with the characteristics of the creator. Initially, it focuses simply on design, which, having been found in the world, indicates this presence of an intelligent Designer. Cleanthes, Philo rightly surmises, now wants to extend the comparison, to conclude that the goodness in the world indicates divine goodness. This aspect of the analogy, however, will not follow if there is also evil and suffering in the world, or so Philo assumes. He believes that Cleanthes shares this assumption, and it is the reason behind his denial of the existence of human misery. Philo seizes this opportunity.

> And is it possible, Cleanthes, said Philo, that after all these reflections, and infinitely more, which might be suggested, you can still persevere in your anthropomorphism, and assert the moral attributes of the Deity, his justice, benevolence, mercy, and rectitude, to be of the same nature with these virtues in human creature? His power we allow is infinite: Whatever he wills is executed: But neither man nor any other animal is happy: Therefore, he does not will their happiness. His wisdom is infinite: He is never mistaken in choosing the means to any ends: But the course of nature tends not to human or animal felicity: Therefore, it is not established for that purpose. . . . Epicurus' old questions are yet unanswered. Is he willing to prevent evil, but not able? then is he impotent. Is he able, but not willing? then is he malevolent. Is he both able and willing? whence then is evil? (DNR 10.24–25)

It is important to observe specifically what Philo is challenging and what conclusion he draws, not only because of the critical place that this part of the conversation places in the *Dialogues* as a whole, but also because his comments have been subject to some poor interpretation. In an often-cited article, Nelson Pike suggests that it is Philo's intent to deny the existence of

God, on the basis of the incompatibility between the proposition *God exists* and *There occur instances of suffering*.[15] However, it is clear from this passage that Philo does not conclude that there is no divine being, rather only that the deity cannot have the kind of moral characteristics that Cleanthes desires to attribute to him.

William Capitan asserts that Philo 'is demolishing natural religion, not by disproving God's existence, but by invalidating the argument to God's moral attributes'.[16] Capitan's analysis is closer to being correct than Pike's, but misleading in one important regard. He is right that natural theologians like the English deists Charles Blount and Matthew Tindal are very optimistic about what can be learned of God's transcendent and moral attributes through natural religion. He is also right to suggest that Hume is critical of this enterprise. Where he is incorrect, however, is in his assertion that Hume (through Philo) is trying to demolish natural religion. If Philo really intended to dismantle natural religion, he would not assert that God's existence can be known through the evidences of design. What Philo really purposes is to *refine* natural theology, so that it only concludes to those things which really can be asserted on the basis of experience. Philo desires to correct and sharpen the conclusions of natural religion, as does Hume. Hume does not disbelieve in the project of natural religion. He simply refuses to take it as far as most natural theologians (including the English deists) do.

What Philo specifically targets is the attempt to conclude to God's goodness on the basis of the good things evident in the world, while ignoring the evidence of human suffering and misery. He will not allow the inference to divine moral goodness from the mixed lot of good and evil in the world. Cleanthes objects, asserting that to take this approach would put an end to all religion. He asks, 'For to what purpose establish the natural attributes of the Deity, while the moral are still doubtful and uncertain?' (DNR 10.28). In fact, it is Philo's goal to do just what Cleanthes thinks is impossible, namely, to establish a true religion which affirms God's transcendent (or 'natural') attributes, but no moral ones.

Philo reiterates that this world is not what we would expect from a combination of infinite power, infinite wisdom and infinite goodness. Given that state of affairs, no one would expect misery. Rhetorically, he allows that pain or misery in humans is at least potentially compatible with omniscience and omnibenevolence in God. It is a possible state of affairs. He does so, however, only to raise the bar for Cleanthes higher than simply demonstrating the *possibility* of this combination. Cleanthes needs to establish the unqualified moral goodness of the deity from the evidence of this world.

Philo is quite sure that it cannot be done, and, indeed, Cleanthes is not equal to the task. On the question of divine goodness, Philo triumphs:

> But there is no view of human life or of the condition of mankind, from which, without the greatest violence, we can infer the moral attributes, or learn that infinite benevolence, conjoined with infinite power and infinite wisdom, which we must discover by the eyes of faith alone. (DNR 10.36)

The philosophical problem that is under consideration here is the famous problem of evil, which includes this *trilemma*, namely that these three propositions cannot all be true together: God is omnibenevolent, God is omnipotent, Evil exists. As Philo noted in DNR 10.25, this trilemma has roots in the thought of Epicurus, who concluded that the tensions in the trilemma mean that there is no God. This challenge, of course, invites a response, and there is a long history of theodicies, which are attempts to resolve the problem of evil. Logically, one may resolve the trilemma by denying one of the three propositions or adding propositions which somehow resolve the tension. Cleanthes denies the existence of evil, while Philo nullifies the goodness of God. Demea opines that the evils of this world will be rectified in a future state (DNR 10.29).

In my judgment, however, the theodicies presented by Demea and Cleanthes do not represent the best philosophical or theological thinking on this most difficult problem. Cleanthes' two contentions that misery does not exist in the world and that God is only finitely perfect (DNR 11.1) are both philosophically deficient. The existence of suffering in the world is ever-present before us, and the notion of 'finite perfection' is of both questionable coherence and religious satisfaction. Demea's theodicy may be a comfort to those who believe in a life to come, but, as Cleanthes notes, such speculations are not part of natural religion or philosophy of religion. The effect of the *Dialogues* to show that the problem of evil truly derails belief in an omnibenevolent god is diminished, in my view, by the absence of the free will defense or the notion that evil is a privation (as presented by Augustine and Aquinas) or even a responsible presentation of Leibniz' best-of-all-possible-worlds theodicy. The failure of Hume to present the best answers to the problem of evil does not, however, change the fundamental point of this investigation, which is that Hume did not believe that one could infer divine moral goodness in the deity on the basis of natural religion.

The strong version of the problem of evil holds that nothing can be done to resolve the tension of the trilemma, except to deny the existence of God.

Epicurus draws this conclusion. However, it must be admitted that the trilemma can be solved if the proposition regarding divine omnibenevolence is denied. This weaker solution to the problem of evil is clearly the point of view that emerges from the *Dialogues*. The fact that most theists are loathe to make this move does not invalidate the logical effectiveness of it. It is this move that Philo makes. He does not deny God's existence, only his goodness.

Philo's thought experiment of the intelligent alien imported to consider the empirical facts of our world concludes that if this being is not already 'antecedently convinced of a supreme intelligent, benevolent and powerful, but is left to gather such a belief from the appearance of things', he will never do so (DNR 11.2). In other words, there is no reason to believe that the imaginary alien will discover even some limited goodness in the creator, given the presence of so much suffering and misery.

Philo also briefly considers the possibility that we live in a universe that is not governed by a single supreme being possessed of infinite goodness, but rather that there is a cosmic dualism, in which there is an ongoing battle between the forces of good and evil. He quickly concludes, however, that there is no reason for asserting this Manichean system, because of the lack of evidence for any transcendent goodness or malice. 'The true conclusion is, that the original source of all things is entirely indifferent to all these principles, and has no more regard to good above ill than to heat above cold, or to drought above moisture, or to light above heavy' (DNR 11.14). Here Philo voices his final conclusion, which is that the deity is morally indifferent. There simply is no evidence for any moral sentiments or tendencies towards good or evil apparent in the deity.

> There may *four* hypotheses be framed concerning the first causes of the universe: *that* they are endowed with perfect goodness, *that* they have perfect malice, *that* they are opposite and have both goodness and malice, *that* they have neither goodness or malice. Mixed phenomena can never prove the two former unmixed principle. And the uniformity and steadiness of the general laws seem to oppose the third. The fourth, therefore, seems by far the most probable. (DNR 11.15)

All that is required of true religionists is simply to know that God exists, and to recognize his transcendent attributes. Philo approvingly quoted Seneca, that to 'know God is to worship him'. Then he adds that 'All other worship is indeed absurd, superstitious, and even impious. It degrades him to the low condition of mankind, who are delighted with entreaty, solicitation, presents and flattery' (DNR 12.31). The only act required of the true religionist is the philosophical understanding that God exists and that he is a single being, possessing superior and surpassing intelligence and power. The limited degree to which he is knowable precludes any further knowledge of his character. He created the universe and governs it through a general providence. The deity, however, is not a moral being, having no moral sentiments that correspond either to the vices or virtues found in humans. This, then, is the nature of Hume's god. All that is left is to consider what name to give to this particular conception of God.

Characterizing Hume's Theism

The last task of this chapter is to characterize the nature of Hume's theism. What name best fits Hume's particular version of belief in God? None of the standard appellations really fit. After the distinction is made between atheism and theism, one finds that typical terms, like polytheism and pantheism, can be quickly dismissed. Deism, whether historical or popular, is not appropriate, either.

Thus, there is a paucity of necessary names to discuss the different possible conceptions of the divine being. It seems to me that our ability to discuss intelligently the range of possibilities regarding the nature of the deity is enhanced if we conceive of the deity as possessing certain characteristics that can be located on a continuum. For instance, a numerical continuum would extend from the belief in a single divine being to the position that there is an infinite number of deities. A power continuum would stretch from very limited power to an infinite degree. On the basis of the investigation just completed, a characterization of Hume's deity would require six such continua: knowability, number, power, intelligence, providence and goodness. Hume's god is also characterized by one action. He is a creator, a role not easily adapted to a continuum.

According to Hume, genuine theism holds that the deity is knowable to only a minimal degree, is one in number, is possessed of infinite power and intelligence, governs only by a general providence and is morally indifferent. Thus, a specific location has been staked out on each of these continua. It should be pointed out that the purpose of these continua is to serve as conceptual tools for making more concrete the differences between abstract characterizations of various attributes. It is no doubt the case that the continua are less helpful for some attributes than for others. It seems to me that the use of a continuum is helpful in considering the moral goodness of a deity, but perhaps less so when considering the number of the deity, since one may wonder where the notion of pantheism resides on that continuum.

What does this conception of the deity make Hume? First of all, it seems that it makes him unique. There is no major religion, important religious thinker or theological trend of which I am aware, that conceives of God in just this way. Clarke's second kind of deist, it may be recalled, also denied divine goodness. However, the distance between Hume and the English deists on so many other issues precludes identifying Hume with this group, which was, in any case, more theoretical than historical.

Thus, a new name is in order. Clearly, the element that makes Hume's system unique is his belief that God is morally indifferent. When one factors in Hume's belief that God is not to be worshiped, but only known philosophically, it is obvious that Hume's conception of the deity is not replicated by any religion or theological system. Hume is not a Christian, nor does he fit in any other religious category. He is, however, a theist, and if a name is needed, perhaps one could name this position *amoral theism,* so long as it is understood the amorality refers to the being who is the object of belief and not to the character of the believer.

Conclusion

The purpose of this book has been to investigate David Hume's conclusions on the existence and nature of God. Here is a summary of Hume's beliefs. There exists a true religion, rooted in genuine theism, and it is distinct from the beliefs and practices of the common person. There is also a false, popular religion, which arises out of certain human propensities and is characterized by either superstitious doctrines and rituals or enthusiastic flights of fancy. True religion, which is a species of true philosophy, grows out of the awe that one feels in recognition of the pervasive evidences for design, purpose and order that are apparent in the universe. This evidence, fostered by good education and philosophical rigor, produces immediate impressions of the existence of the divine creator and his transcendent perfections. Popular religion is plagued by fluctuating cycles, in which the vulgar religionists may happen upon some religious truths (such as the belief in one god) in the heat of their enthusiastic exaltations, but these beliefs are only coincidental with true religion. They are not based on discursive thought, and eventually cycle back into superstitious polytheism and idolatry. True religion, being a species of true philosophy, is a rare occurrence and only a small number of people are true religionists. True religion holds to a general, not a particular, providence, and tends towards a view of the deity which emphasizes his otherness and distinctiveness from human beings. True worship of this divine being is nothing more than knowledge of him, and there are no religious duties or other practical consequences that are derived from this belief. Belief in true religion does not lead to a religious foundation for morality, nor a belief in an afterlife. The only act required of the true religionist is the philosophical understanding that God exists and that he is a single being, possessing superior and surpassing intelligence and power. The limited degree to which he is knowable precludes any further knowledge of his character. He created the universe and governs it through a general providence. The deity, however, is not a moral being, having no moral sentiments that correspond either to the vices or virtues found in humans.

Two implications, it seems to me, are apparent from this project of examining Hume's theism. The first is one that has been repeated throughout, namely that the present understanding of Hume on God is incorrect. I hope that this book will help to correct the errors of the conventional story and to overcome the conclusion that Hume is an unqualified secularist and unmitigated religious iconoclast. The correct interpretation of a great philosopher is sufficient justification in and of itself, and my hope is that this project has moved Hume scholarship closer to that ideal.

A further implication, however, presents itself to me, and it serves to explain why I believe this book to be more than simply a historical corrective. I do not subscribe to all the conclusions that Hume has drawn regarding God and religion. My own convictions lay with the classic formulations of historical Protestant Christianity. However, I believe that the example of David Hume is instructive regarding the great questions of religion and philosophy. Human beings have always wondered about the possibility that there is a supernatural being who transcends our own world, our own universe. Countless religious traditions and an unending stream of philosophers have weighed in on this all-important question. As a people, we are far from a consensus, if indeed that is what we seek.

But few have subjected the question of God and the practice of religion to such a searching inquiry, and with such mental acuity, as has David Hume. Others, like Friedrich Nietzsche or Sigmund Freud or Bertrand Russell, have arrived at more skeptical conclusions, and perhaps Hume desired to reach the same atheistic conclusions as the 19th century Germans and the 20th century Logical Positivists, but, the fact is that he did not do so. This observation carries with it meaningful implications regarding the viability of religious belief in an intellectual world. Certainly, Hume's belief in the existence of God is not sufficient for the truthfulness of the proposition that God exists. It is, however, an important consideration for those who wish to advance a secular and naturalistic worldview, namely that one of history's greatest religious critics was never able to escape the conclusion that a divine being exists. Indeed, the truth of the matter is (in Hume's own words) that 'the whole frame of nature bespeaks an intelligent author; and no rational enquirer can, after serious reflection, suspend his belief a moment with regard to the primary principles of genuine Theism and Religion.' Thus, the testimony of one of history's great skeptics and thinkers is that there is a god – a sobering message to a secular age.

Notes

Chapter 1

[1] Wilson (1999), pages 23, 25.

[2] Hecht (2003), pages 347–348.

[3] Boswell's record of this conversation with Hume is recorded in Kemp Smith (1947), page 76–79.

[4] The first sentence of J. C. A. Gaskin (1988) reads thus, 'In the totality of his work Hume wrote more about religion than about any other single philosophical subject.' Gaskin offers no statistical evidence, but the conclusion seems plausible.

[5] 'My Own Life' can be found in Mossner (1980), which is considered the standard biography of Hume (pages 611–615).

[6] Compare, for instance, the offering by Barry Stroud (1977) in the prestigious *Arguments of the Philosophers* series which purports to be general introductions to the thought of influential philosophers. In the Preface, Stroud announces: 'In this book I try to provide a comprehensive interpretation of Hume's philosophy.' In the next paragraph, however, he admits that he says nothing about religion (page ix). Other examples of this neglect of Hume's philosophy of religion include Pears (1990), which, despite its title, only discusses Book 1 of the *Treatise*, and Passmore (1980, first published in 1952), which similarly ignores Hume's philosophy of religion.

[7] All citations to Hume's writings will be made in text. See the Abbreviations page for a legend to these citations.

[8] Ayer (1980), pages 95–96.

[9] Price (1965), page 139.

[10] Ibid. page 141.

[11] Penelhum (1975), page 166.

[12] Hume uses a variety of terms to speak of God: the deity, the divine, the creator. I will regard them as synonyms for that transcendent being identified with the creator of the universe. When this being is named specifically, I will capitalize the name (God). When speaking of the species of divine beings (as in the sentence in which this footnote appears), I will speak of a *god*.

[13] One ironic twist regarding Flew is that after a half-century of vigorously defending atheism, Flew has changed his mind regarding the existence of God. In his most recent book, entitled *There is a God* (2007), Flew acknowledges that recent evidence regarding intelligent design has led him to believe there is a deity. At no point in this book, however, does he suggest that he has revised his interpretation of Hume on God.

[14] Flew (1992), page vii.

[15] Flew (1984b), pages 13–14. See also Flew (1984a), pages 62–68 and Flew (1997), pages 410–416.

[16] Flew (1984b), pages 20–23.

[17] Flew (1984a), page 63.

[18] Flew, (1984b), pages 31–33.

[19] 'The Ethics of Belief' by W. K. Clifford (1999) was originally published by *The Contemporary Review* in 1877. The quoted citation is from Madigan, page 77.

[20] Flew (1984b), page 35.

[21] Flew (1984b), pages 43–45.

[22] Flew (1986), page 61.

[23] Flew (1961), page 167.

[24] Ibid. pages 167–169.

[25] Flew (1984a), page 63; Flew (1984b), page 29; Flew (1971), pages 181–182; Flew (1986), page 67.

[26] Flew (1997), page 414.

[27] Flew (1986), page 67.

[28] Flew (1961), page 239. See also Flew (1992), page vii where Flew includes the descriptor 'complete unbeliever'.

[29] Warnock (1958), page 164. Cited by Flew (1961), page 238.

[30] Flew (1961), page 192.

[31] Flew (1999), page 195.

[32] Flew (1984b), pages 45–47. See also EHU 11.1.11.

[33] Flew (1961), page 215.

[34] Gaskin (1988), page 1.

[35] Ibid. page 6.

[36] Ibid. pages 6–7.

[37] The term is not Hume's, but was coined by Kemp Smith in Kemp Smith (1941), pages 446–458. Hume more often uses the terms *propensity* or *instinct.*

[38] Gaskin (1993), page 319.

[39] Cf. Livingston (1986), pages 33–73.

[40] Livingston (1986), page 61. See also pages 42–44.

[41] This position is defended in the last chapter of Gaskin (1988), and Gaskin (1983), pages 160–173.

[42] Gaskin (1983), page 163. Cf. Andre (1993), pages 141–142 for a similar attempt to try to differentiate between levels of belief and unbelief with regard to the deity.

[43] Gaskin (1983), page 164.

[44] Ibid. pages 162–163, 166.

[45] Ibid. page 171. On the same page, he describes Hume's position as 'something like the conclusion of deism shorn of reliance upon *proofs* and hence diffidently affirmed: order in the natural world suggests an origin or source which might warrant cautious use of the word intelligence.'

[46] Ibid. pages 167–169.

[47] Ibid. page 161.

[48] See, for example, Sire (2004) for an example of this contemporary expression of deism on pages 45–58, which he nevertheless conflates with historical deism.

[49] Clarke (1732), pages 159–174.

[50] Yandell (1990), page 25. On the same page, Yandell refers to Hume's theism as 'diaphanous'.

Chapter 2

[1] For more on Hume's skepticism, see Livingston (1984), Norton (1982) and Schmidt (2003).

[2] Millican (2002), page 417.

[3] Booth (1974) observes that 'There is reason to believe that most of us think we are less vulnerable to mistakes with irony than we are. If we have enjoyed many ironies and observed less experienced readers making fools of themselves, we can hardly resist flattering ourselves for making our way pretty well. But the truth is that even highly sophisticated readers often go astray' (page 1).

[4] Millican (2002), page 449.

[5] Price (1965), page 141.

[6] M. A. Stewart on page 91, Justin Broakes on page 200, George Botterill on page 289 and Don Garrett on page 328 all identify a particular passage from Hume as ironic with little or no supporting argumentation in Millican (2002).

[7] Kemp Smith (1947), pages 68–75.

[8] Pike (1985), pages 207–222.

[9] Penelhum (1975), pages 191–196.

[10] Mossner (1977), pages 1–2. He does not cite his source for this definition, but it is in proximate conformity to the definition given in the 1971 edition of the *Oxford English Dictionary*.

[11] Ibid. page 4.

[12] Fowler (1987) makes the same distinction, calling the two types *situational* and *verbal* irony (page 129). Cf. also Abrams (1993) on verbal irony (page 97).

[13] Price (1965). On page 7, there is cosmic irony and the irony which is the opposite of what is said. On page 25, Price mentions philosophical irony and Socratic irony, while pages 32–33 give us quantitative and tonic irony. On page 37, he discusses 'conduct of the argument' or on the whole irony, both/and irony and blame-by-praise irony. Two further unnamed kinds of irony are mentioned on page 87. Almost certainly, Price did not intend the reader to see each of these items as different types of irony. Several of these 'types' may in fact be examples of the same sort of irony. However, he provides no overall summary or classification of the different types of irony, so there is no way to be sure how many kinds of irony Price thinks there are.

[14] Ibid. page 102.

[15] Ibid. page 109.

[16] Ibid. page 33.

[17] Ibid. page 82.

[18] Cicero (1975), pages 110–111. See also Knox (1961), page 5.

[19] Quintilian (2001), pages 4.58–4.59.

[20] Knox (1961), page 6.

[21] These items are part of what Knox calls 'the dictionary.' He provides extensive examples and discussion on pages 38–98.

[22] Knox (1961), pages 58–59. Other classifications that Knox distinguishes are Saying the Contrary for the Purpose of Emphasis, Understatement, Indirection, Elaborate Fiction (an extended story, like *Candide*), Spoof, Derisive or Mocking Attack, and Dramatic Irony (employing a 'dupe' or 'ingenu' like the lead character in *Forrest Gump*).

[23] Muecke (1980), page 19.

[24] Ibid. pages 19–20.

[25] Ibid. page 20.

[26] Voltaire (1947), page 25. Cf. Muecke (1980), pages 14–15.

[27] Muecke (1980), page 23.

[28] Ibid. pages 52–60.

[29] Ibid. page 60.

[30] Ibid. page 56.

[31] Quintilian (2001), pages 3.456–3.457.

[32] Booth (1974), pages 5–7.

[33] Ibid. pages 240–241.

[34] Ibid. pages 10–13. I have reworded his steps in order to make them more precise.

[35] Ibid. pages 49–76.

[36] A good example is a 1751 letter to his friend, Dr John Clephane in which Hume gently chastises his friend for not writing sooner, but resolves to forgive Clephane 'to keep myself in a proper disposition for saying the Lord's Prayer, whenever I find space enough for it' (L 70; 1.148).

[37] Kierkegaard (1989), page 248.

[38] Mossner (1980), page 234. Cf. letter to Gilbert Elliot (L 71; 1.153).

[39] Swift (1973), pages 502–509.

[40] Ibid. page 503.

[41] Ibid. page 504.

[42] The benefits of this proposal are first discussed on page 503 and again on page 507.

[43] Ibid. page 505.

[44] Ibid. page 508.

[45] Ibid. One of these essays is identified by Greenberg and Piper as his 'Proposal for the Universal Use of Irish Manufactures'. See footnote 3 on page 508.

[46] Box (1990), pages 206–225.

[47] Ibid. page 209. In a footnote to this passage (#55), Box mentions Mossner (1990), Gaskin (1988) and Penelhum (1986) as failed attempts to discern precisely what Hume meant by the phrase *true religion*. Notably absent from this list are Livingston (1984) and (1986), which attempt this very project.

[48] Ibid. page 211.

[49] Ibid. page 212.

[50] Ibid.

[51] Ibid. page 213.

[52] Rivers (2000), page 2.37.

[53] See the Author's Advertisement to *Alciphron* in Berkeley (1993), pages 17–18.

[54] Shaftesbury (2001), page 1.46. Shaftesbury also defends this 'defensive raillery' on pages 1.41–1.44.

[55] Berman (1987), pages 66–67.

[56] Ibid. pages 72–73.

[57] Rivers (2000), page 2.40.

[58] Fieser (1995), pages 431–449.

[59] Ibid. page 439. The original quotation is from William Warburton's *Remarks* (1757).

[60] Ibid. page 439. The original quotation is from George Horne's *Letters on Infidelity* (1784).

[61] Hume continues his discussion of satire at length in this section and the next. He compares the difference between a person who 'openly abuses me' and the one who 'slyly intimates his contempt' to the difference between an impression and an idea. The explicit insult (like the impression) is conceived 'with greater force', whereas the subtle irony resembles the idea in that it is 'more feeble', but also a mark of greater respect in that it shows more consideration to the person (T 1.3.13.14).

[62] Mossner (1980) mentions a number of more liberal-minded or moderate members of the clergy in Edinburgh who were friends of Hume, for example, Hugh Blair, Alexander Carlyle, John Home and others (page 274).

[63] Perhaps the only time that Hume engaged in 'pamphleteering' is *A Letter from a Gentleman*. But even this letter is mild in tone compared with the work of the freethinkers.

[64] Stephen (1902), page 1.86.

Chapter 3

[1] See Mounce (1999), pages 106–107, and Millican (2002), pages 36–37.

[2] O'Connor (2001), pages 10–11. See also pages 14 and 206–212.

[3] The quotation is from Hefelbower (1920), page 217, and the second article is Winnett (1960).

[4] Rowe (2000), page 853.

[5] Daniel-Rops (1964), page 63.

[6] Hefelbower (1920) categorically states that there is no foundation at all for reading philosophical deism back onto the Deists, who 'scarcely even touched philosophical problems,' (page 217). While this may be overstating the case a bit, Hefelbower's frustration is justified. Winnett (1960) carefully spells out the same distinction between popular (or philosophical) deism and historical deism and also provides some more examples of scholars who conflate the two (pages 70–71).

[7] Gaskin (1988), page 221.

[8] See Mossner (1980), page 483. For other accounts and interpretations, see Gay (1966), pages 400–401 and Hecht (2003), page 352.

[9] Gaskin (1983), page 165. The story is from Mossner (1980), page 485.

[10] Voltaire (1962), page 438. See the 2nd question under the entry 'Religion'.

[11] Gaskin (1983), page166.

[12] Clarke's Boyle Lectures were eventually published together in a number of editions, the 8th and last as Clarke (1732).

[13] Clarke (1732), page 159.

[14] Gaskin (1988) writes, 'I shall call the "plain, philosophical assent" to the existence of a god as indicated by the vestiges of the design argument, *a god whose sole attribute is an intelligence* which may bear some remote analogy to the intelligence of man, "attenuated deism".' (page 223 italics added). For Gaskin, attenuated deism describes a deity whose sole attribute is some kind of intelligence that is higher than human intelligence.

[15] Clarke (1732), page 161.

[16] Ibid. pages 164–165.

[17] Ibid. pages 167–168.

[18] Ibid. page 170.

[19] This list reflects only thinkers who had a hand in the English intellectual debates. Continental thinkers like Spinoza, Pascal, Bayle, Malebranche, Diderot, d'Alembert and others could readily be added.

[20] Two excellent books on this relatively obscure, but historically very significant, movement are van Leeuwen (1963) and Shapiro (1983).

[21] Burns (1981), pages 12–16.

[22] Ibid. pages 108–109. Burns also gives one of the better accounts of the intellectual complexity of this era, pages 9–46.

[23] Berkeley (1993), pages 98–113.

[24] Brown (1990), pages 209–212.

[25] Reventlow (1985), page 289.

[26] Ibid. page 289.

[27] Hefelbower (1920), page 219.

[28] Stromberg (1954), pages 56–69.

[29] Cherbury (1937), page 289.

[30] Ibid. pages 291–296.

[31] Reventlow (1985), page 188.

[32] Cherbury (1937), pages 298–300.

[33] See Orr (1934), pages 67–69, and Reventlow (1985), pages 188–193.

[34] Orr (1934), page 110.

[35] Stephen (1902), page 1.194.

[36] Popkin (1999), page 441.

[37] Stephen (1902), pages 1.101–1.102.

[38] Toland (1997), page 36.

[39] Ibid. pages 67–68 and also Reventlow (1985), pages 298–301.

[40] Shaftesbury (1999), pages 2.30–2.44.

[41] Reventlow (1985), pages 311–318.

[42] Since Locke was an acquaintance of Shaftesbury, Blount, Collins and Toland, and the English deists were greatly influenced by him, it is sometimes supposed that Locke was a deist. This topic is treated thoroughly by S. G. Hefelbower (1918), a book which serves, in part, as a model for this chapter. Hefelbower concludes that Locke was not a deist, because he embraced the cosmological arguments (instead

of the teleological argument favored by the English deists), he accepted the existence of miracles, and he also believed in supernatural written revelation (pages 172–175). None of these items fits the profile of English deism.

[43] Collins (1713), pages 33–34.

[44] Orr (1934), pages 130–134.

[45] Reventlow (1985), page 359.

[46] Orr (1934), pages 138–140 and Stephen (1902), pages 1.130–1.134.

[47] Reventlow (1985), page 376.

[48] Tindal (1730), page 107.

[49] Thus, Hume would follow the English deist agenda on only points 6, 9, 10, 11 and 12, the last four of which are items that the English deists debated.

[50] O'Higgins (1971), page 493. Gawlick (1977) challenges this analysis.

[51] Philip Skelton's two-volume *Ophiomaches, or Deism Revealed* (1749) is a series of eight dialogues on English deism.

[52] Probably the best 18th century analysis of deism is John Leland's *A View of the Principal Deistical Writers* (1754). Leland calls Hume a deist because he shares some deist positions, despite the substantial differences between Hume and the English deists. Hume observed to a friend, 'My Compliments to Dr Leland, & tell him, that he certainly has mistaken my character.' (NL 25.43)

[53] Although Gawlick (1977), mentions (page 128) some historians who have called Hume a deist, the overwhelming majority of historians that I have read have concluded that Hume was not a deist. Historians who have concluded that Hume was not a deist include: Stromberg (1954), pages 54, 67–68; Gay (1966), page 413; Burns (1981), page 13; O'Higgins (1971), pages 492–501; Gonzalez (1985), page 190; Latourette (1975), page 1004; Walker (1969), page 440; Durants (1965), page 160; Brown (1990), page 211; Badia Cabrera (2001), pages 184–185; Orr (1934), page 166; Mossner (1980), page 113; and Waring (1967), pages xv–xvi. Neither Copleston (1959), Reventlow (1985) nor Stephen (1902) in their detailed analyses of English deism mention or identify Hume as a deist.

[54] Mossner (1980), page 395.

Chapter 4

[1] Kemp Smith (1947), page 11.

[2] Mossner (1990), page 113.

[3] Box (1990), page 209.

[4] Mossner (1980), page 321.

[5] Cited in ibid. pages 325–326.

[6] The review by A. Marvel is republished in Tweyman (1996), pages 201–205. Mossner (1980) cites the same quotation, but attributes to a different source (pages 331–332).

[7] Falkenstein (2003), page 7.

[8] Ibid. pages 12–13.

[9] I take the phrases 'vulgar religion' and 'popular religion' to be synonymous in Hume, and I employ them interchangeably as well. Of course, the word *vulgar*

in this context does not mean obscene as it does today, but it carries the 18th century meaning of common, or that which characterizes uneducated individuals or unsophisticated thought.

[10] Cf. Tweyman (1996) for similar examples of disdain by contemporary theological conservatives towards Hume's arguments (pages 201–203, 208–209, 234–235, 245–248).

[11] For a similar analysis, see Schmidt (2003), page 361.

[12] The oft-cited letter to Gilbert Elliot of Minto, dated March 10, 1751, provides valuable, and yet tantalizingly vague hints at the intentions behind the *Dialogues* (L 72; 1.153–1.157).

[13] Gaskin (1988), pages 210–213 and Sessions (1991), page 30.

[14] Sessions (1991), page 30.

[15] Hendel (1925), page 270.

[16] Yandell (1990), page 37.

[17] Badia Cabrera (2001), page 255.

[18] Sessions (2002), page 209.

[19] Kemp Smith (1947), pages 64–66.

[20] Wadia (1976), pages 283–284.

[21] Pike (1985), page 229.

[22] See also Tweyman (1986), chapters 3–4 and Logan (1993), chapters 5–6.

[23] Badia Cabrera (2001), pages 94–104.

[24] Kemp Smith (1947), page 28.

[25] Pike (1985), page 233.

[26] Sessions (2002), page 173.

[27] Badia Cabrera (2001), page 284.

[28] Parent (1976), pages 63–68.

[29] Pike (1985), pages 223–224.

[30] Gaskin (1993), page 321–322.

[31] Box (1990), page 209.

[32] Buckle (2001), pages 276–277 and Jeffner (1966), page 195. I will distinguish 'Hume' the interlocutor in quotes from Hume the author.

Chapter 5

[1] Huxley (1879), pages 144–145.

[2] Capaldi (1970), page 233.

[3] Jeffner (1966), pages 193–196.

[4] Ibid. page 180.

[5] Ibid. page 198.

[6] Grudem (1994), page 315.

[7] George (1988), pages 204–213.

[8] Leland (1836), page 268.

[9] Ibid. pages 269–270.

[10] Calvin (1960), pages 1.201–1.202.

[11] George (1988), page 210.

[12] Winship (1996), pages 38–39.

[13] Ibid. pages 41–42.
[14] Ibid. pages 43, 44.
[15] Pike (1963), page 86. Pike repeats his assessment that Philo concludes atheism on pages 87, 97 and 101.
[16] Capitan (1966), page 82.

Bibliography

Primary Sources

Berkeley, George (1732), *Alciphron in Focus* (edited by David Berman). London: Routledge, 1993.

Blount, Charles (1680), *The First Two Books of Philostratus, concerning the Life of Apollonius*. London.

Butler, Joseph (1736), *The Analogy of Religion Natural and Revealed to the Constitution and Course of Nature*. London: George Routledge and Sons, 1887.

Calvin, John (1559), *Institutes of the Christian Religion* (edited by John T. McNeill). Philadelphia, PA: The Westminster Press, 1960.

Cherbury, Lord Herbert of (1624), *De Veritate* (translated by Meyrick H. Carré). Bristol: J. W. Arrowsmith Ltd. 1937.

Cicero *De Officiis* (translated by Walter Miller). Cambridge: Cambridge University Press, (1975).

Clarke, Samuel (1732), *Discourse concerning the Being and Attributes of God, the Obligations of Natural Religion and the Truth and Certainty of the Christian Revelation* (8th edition). London.

Clifford, W. K. *The Ethics of Belief and Other Essays* (edited by Timothy J. Madigan). Amherst, NY: Prometheus Books, 1999.

Collins, Anthony (1713), *An Essay concerning the Use of Reason in Propositions: A Discourse of Free-Thinking*. London.

—(1724), *A Discourse on the Grounds and Reasons of the Christian Religion*. London.

Horne, George (1784), *Letters on Infidelity*. Oxford.

Kierkegaard, Soren (1841), *The Concept of Irony* (edited and translated by Howard V. Hong and Edna H. Hong). Princeton, NJ: Princeton University Press, 1989.

Locke, John (1695), *The Reasonableness of Christianity* (edited by John C. Higgins-Biddle). Oxford: Clarendon Press, 1999.

Quintilian *The Orator's Education* (edited and translated by Donald A. Russell). Cambridge: Harvard University Press, 2001.

Shaftesbury (Third Earl of), Anthony Ashley Cooper (1732), *Characteristicks of Men, Manner, Opinions, Times*. Indianapolis, IN: Liberty Fund, 2001.

Swift, Jonathan *The Writings of Jonathan Swift* (edited by Robert A. Greenberg and William B. Piper). New York: Norton, 1973.

Tindal, Matthew (1730), *Christianity as Old as the Creation*. London.

Toland, John (1696), *John Toland's Christianity Not Mysterious* (edited by Philip McGuinness, Alan Harrison and Richard Kearney). Dublin: The Lilliput Press, 1997.

—(1721), *Pantheisticon*. London.

Voltaire (1761), *Candide* (trans. by John Butt). London: Penguin, 1947.

—(1769), *Philosophical Dictionary* (translated by Peter Gay). New York: Harcourt, Brace and World, 1962.

Warburton, William (1757), *Remarks on Mr. David Hume's Essay on the Natural History of Religion*. London.

Wollaston, William (1750), *Religion of Nature Delineated* (8th edition). London.

Secondary Sources

Abrams, M. H. (1993), *A Glossary of Literary Terms* (6th edition). Fort Worth, TX: Harcourt Brace College Publishers.

Andre, Shane (1993), 'Was Hume an atheist?'. *Hume Studies*, 19, 141–166.

Ayer, A. J. (1980), *Hume*. New York: Hill and Wang.

Badia Cabrera, Miguel A. (2001), *Hume's Reflection on Religion*. Dordrecht: Kluwer.

Berman, David (1987), 'Deism, immortality and the art of theological lying' in Lemay (1987).

—(1988), *A History of Atheism in Britain*. London: Croom Helm.

Booth, Wayne C. (1974), *A Rhetoric of Irony*. Chicago, IL: University of Chicago Press.

Box, M. A. (1990), *The Suasive Art of David Hume*. Princeton, NJ: Princeton University Press.

Brown, Colin (1990), *From the Ancient World to the Age of Enlightenment*. Downers Grove, IL: InterVarsity Press.

Buckle, Stephen (2001), *Hume's Enlightenment Tract*. Oxford: Clarendon Press.

Burns, R. M. (1981), *The Great Debate on Miracles*. Lewisburg, PA: Bucknell University Press.

Capaldi, Nicholas (1970), 'Hume's philosophy of religion: God without ethics'. *International Journal for Philosophy of Religion*, 1, 233–240.

—(1992), 'The dogmatic slumber of Hume scholarship'. *Hume Studies*, 18, 117–135.

Capitan, W. H. (1966), 'Part X of Hume's Dialogues'. *American Philosophical Quarterly*, 3, 82–86.

Copleston, Frederick, S. J. (1959), *Hobbes to Hume* (Volume V of *A History of Philosophy*). New York: Image Books.

Craig, Edward, editor (2000), *Routledge Encyclopedia of Philosophy*. London: Routledge.

Daniel-Rops, Henri (1964), *The Church of the Eighteenth Century* (Volume 7 of *History of the Church of Christ*). Garden City, NY: Image Books.

Durant, Will and Ariel (1965), *The Age of Voltaire* (Volume 9 of *The Story of Civilization*). New York: Simon and Schuster.

Falkenstein, Lorne (2003), 'Hume's project in "The natural history of religion"'. *Religious Studies*, 39, 1–21.

Fieser, James (1995), 'Hume's concealed attack on religion and his early critics'. *Journal of Philosophical Research*, 20, 431–449.

—(2001), (ed.) *Early Responses to Hume's Writings on Religion* (2 volumes). Bristol, England: Thoemmes Press.

Flew, Antony (1961), *Hume's Philosophy of Belief*. London: Routledge and Kegan Paul.

—(1971), *An Introduction to Western Philosophy*. Indianapolis, IN: Bobbs-Merrill.

—(1984a), *God: A Critical Enquiry*. La Salle, IL: Open Court.

—(1984b), *God, Freedom and Immortality*. Buffalo, NY: Prometheus.

—(1986), *David Hume: Philosopher of Moral Science*. New York: Blackwell.

— (1992), (ed.) *Writings on Religion*. La Salle, IL: Open Court.

—(1997), 'The presumption of atheism' in Quinn and Taliaferro (1997).

—(1999), 'Can religion be rational?' in Phillips and Tessin (1999).

—(2007), *There is a God*. New York: HarperOne.

Fowler, Roger (1987), (ed.) *A Dictionary of Modern Critical Terms* (2nd edition). London: Routledge.

Gaskin, J. C. A. (1983), 'Hume's attenuated deism'. *Archiv fur Geschichte der Philosophie*, 65, 160–173.

—(1988), *Hume's Philosophy of Religion* (2nd edition). Atlantic Highlands, NJ: Humanities Press International.

—(1993), 'Hume on religion' in Norton (1993).

Gawlick, Gunter (1977), 'Hume and the deists: a reconsideration' in Morice (1977).

Gay, Peter (1966), *The Enlightenment: An Interpretation: The Rise of Modern Paganism*. New York: Norton.

George, Timothy (1988), *Theology of the Reformers*. Nashville, TN: Broadman.

Gonzalez, Justo L. (1985), *The Reformation to the Present Day*. New York: HarperCollins.

Grudem, Wayne (1994), *Systematic Theology*. Grand Rapids, MI: Zondervan.

Hall, Roland (1978), *Fifty Years of Hume Scholarship: A Bibliographical Guide*. Edinburgh: Edinburgh University Press.

Hecht, Jennifer Michael (2003), *Doubt: A History*. New York: HarperCollins.

Hefelbower, S. G. (1918), *The Relation of John Locke to English Deism*. Chicago, IL: The University of Chicago Press.

—(1920), 'Deism historically defined'. *American Journal of Theology*, 24, 217–223.

Hendel, Charles William (1963), *Studies in the Philosophy of David Hume*. Indianapolis, IN: Bobbs-Merrill.

Hester, Marcus (1986), (ed.) *Hume's Philosophy of Religion*. Winston-Salem, NC: Wake Forest University Press.

Huxley, Thomas (1879), *Hume*. New York: Harper & Brothers.

Jeffner, Anders (1966), *Butler and Hume on Religion*. Stockholm: Diakonistyrelsens bokforlag.

Kemp Smith, Norman (1941), *The Philosophy of David Hume*. London: MacMillan.

—(1947), (ed.) *Dialogues concerning Natural Religion*. Indianapolis, IN: Bobbs-Merrill.

Knox, Norman (1961), *The Word Irony and its Context, 1500–1755*. Durham, NC: Duke University Press.

Latourette, Kenneth Scott (1975), *A History of Christianity: Volume II, A.D. 1500 – A.D. 1975* (revised). New York: Harper & Row.

Leland, John (1836), *A View of the Principal Deistical Writers that Have Appeared in England during the Last Two Centuries with Observations upon Them* (4th edition). London: Thomas Allman.

Lemay, J. A. Leo (1987), (ed.) *Deism, Masonry and the Enlightenment.* Newark, DE: University of Delaware Press.

Livingston, Donald W. (1984), *Hume's Philosophy of Common Life.* Chicago, IL: University of Chicago Press.

—(1986), 'Hume's conception of true religion' in Hester (1986).

—(1998), *Philosophical Melancholy and Delirium.* Chicago, IL: University of Chicago Press.

Logan, Beryl (1993), *A Religion without Talking.* New York: Peter Lang.

Millican, Peter (2002), (ed.) *Reading Hume on Human Understanding.* Oxford: Oxford University Press.

Morice, G. P.(1977), (ed.) *David Hume: Bicentenary Papers.* Austin, TX: University of Texas Press.

Mossner, Ernest Campbell (1977), 'Hume and the legacy of the Dialogues' in Morice (1977).

—(1980), *The Life of David Hume* (2nd edition). Oxford: Oxford University Press.

—(1990), 'The religion of David Hume' in Yolton (1990).

Mounce, H. O. (1999), *Hume's Naturalism.* London: Routledge.

Muecke, D. C. (1980), *The Compass of Irony* (2nd edition). London: Methuen.

Norton, David Fate, Nicholas Capaldi and Wade L. Robison (1976), (eds) *McGill Hume Studies.* San Diego, CA: Austin Hill Press.

Norton, David Fate (1982), *David Hume: Common-Sense Moralist, Sceptical Metaphysician.* Princeton, NJ: Princeton University Press.

Norton, David Fate (1993), (ed.) *The Cambridge Companion to Hume.* Cambridge: Cambridge University Press.

O'Connor, David (2001), *Routledge Philosophy Guidebook to Hume on Religion.* London: Routledge.

O'Higgins, James (1971), 'Hume and the deists: a contrast in religious approaches'. *Journal of Theological Studies,* 22, 479–501.

Orr, John (1934), *English Deism: Its Roots and its Fruits.* Grand Rapids, MI: Eerdmans.

Parent, William A. (1976), 'Philo's confession'. *Philosophical Quarterly,* 26, 63–68.

Passmore, John (1980), *Hume's Intentions* (3rd edition). London: Duckworth.

Pears, David (1990), *Hume's System.* New York: Oxford University Press.

Penelhum, Terence (1975), *Hume.* London: MacMillan.

—(1986), 'Natural belief and religious belief in Hume's philosophy'. *Philosophical Quarterly,* 33, 166–181.

Phillips, D. Z. and Timothy Tessin (1999), (eds) *Religion and Hume's Legacy.* Claremont, CA: Claremont Graduate School.

Pike, Nelson (1963), 'Hume on evil'. *Philosophical Review,* 72, 180–197.

—(1985), *Hume: Dialogues concerning Natural Religion.* New York: MacMillan.

Popkin, Richard (1999), (ed.) *The Pimlico History of Western Philosophy.* London: Pimlico.

Price, John Valdimir (1965), *The Ironic Hume.* Austin, TX: University of Texas Press.

Quinn, Philip L. and Taliaferro, Charles (1997), (eds) *A Companion to Philosophy of Religion*. London: Blackwell.

Reventlow, Henning Graf (1985), *The Authority of the Bible and the Rise of the Modern World* (translated by John Bowden). Philadelphia, PA: Fortress Press.

Rivers, Isabel (2000), *Reason, Grace and Sentiment* (2 volumes). Cambridge: Cambridge University Press.

Rowe, William (2000), 'Deism' in Craig (2000).

Schmidt, Claudia (2003), *David Hume: Reason in History*. University Park, PA: The Pennsylvania State University Press.

Sessions, William Lad (1991), 'A dialogic interpretation of Hume's Dialogues'. *Hume Studies*, 17, 15–39.

—(2002), *Reading Hume's Dialogues*. Bloomington, IN: Indiana University Press.

Shapiro, Barbara J. (1983), *Probability and Certainty in Seventeenth-Century England*. Princeton, NJ: Princeton, University Press.

Sire, James W. (2004), *The Universe Next Door* (4th edition). Downers Grove, IL: InterVarsity Press.

Skelton, Philip (1990), *Ophiomaches: Or Deism Revealed* (2 Volumes). Bristol, England: Thoemmes Antiquarian Books.

Stephen, Sir Leslie (1902), *History of English Thought in the 18th Century* (3rd edition, 2 volumes). London: John Murray.

Stromberg, Roland N. (1954), *Religious Liberalism in Eighteenth-Century England*. Oxford: Oxford University Press.

Stroud, Barry (1977), *Hume*. London: Routledge.

Tweyman, Stanley (1986), *Scepticism and Belief in Hume's Dialogues concerning Natural Religion*. Dordrecht: Martinus Nijhoff Publishers.

Tweyman, Stanley (1996), (ed.) *Hume on Natural Religion*. Bristol, England: Thoemmes Press.

Van Leeuwen, Henry G. (1963), *The Problem of Certainty in English Thought: 1630–1690)*. The Hague: Martinus Nijhoff.

Wadia, Pheroze S. (1976), 'Philo confounded' in Norton et al. (1976).

Walker, Williston (1970), *A History of Christian Church* (3rd edition). New York: Charles Scribner's Sons.

Waring, E. Graham (1967), (ed.) *Deism and Natural Religion*. New York: Frederick Ungar Publishing.

Warnock, G. J. (1958), *English Philosophy since 1900*. London: Oxford University Press.

Wilson, A. N. (1999), *God's Funeral*. New York: Ballantine Books.

Winnett, A. R. (1960), 'Were the Deists "Deists"?'. *The Church Quarterly Review*, 161, 70–77.

Winship, Michel P. (1996), *Seers of God*. Baltimore, MD: The Johns Hopkins University Press.

Yandell, Keith E. (1990), *Hume's 'Inexplicable Mystery'*. Philadelphia, PA: Temple University Press.

Yolton, John (1990), (ed.) *Philosophy, Religion and Science in the Seventeenth and Eighteenth Centuries*. Rochester, NY: University of Rochester Press.

Index